D1557279

TO
HEAL
THE SOUL

TO
HEAL
THE SOUL

The Spiritual Journal of a Chasidic Rebbe

RABBI KALONYMUS KALMAN SHAPIRA

Son of Rabbi Elimelekh of Grodzisk
Son-in-Law of Rabbi Yerachmiel Moshe of Kozhnitz

translated and edited by
Yehoshua Starrett

JASON ARONSON INC.
Northvale, New Jersey
London

This book was set in 12 point Garamond by TechType of Upper Saddle River, New Jersey, and printed by Book-mart Press in North Bergen, New Jersey.

10 9 8 7 6 5 4 3 2 1

Library of Congress Cataloging-in-Publication Data

Kalonimus Klemish ben Elimelekh, 1889–1944.
   To heal the soul : the spiritual journal of a Chasidic rebbe / translated and edited by Yehoshua Starrett.
      p. cm.
   Includes index.
   ISBN 1-56821-306-9
   1. Hasidism.   2. Spiritual life—Judaism.   3. Jewish meditations.
   I. Starrett, Yehoshua.   II. Title.
   BM198.K33   1995   94-24519
   296.8'332—dc20

Manufactured in the United States of America. Jason Aronson Inc. offers books and cassettes. For information and catalog write to Jason Aronson Inc., 230 Livingston Street, Northvale, New Jersey 07647.

In the ruins of the Warsaw Ghetto, a fragmentary diary was found that records the inner life of the martyred Rebbe of Peasetzna. The Rebbe was the last great educator toward chasidic illumination for young and old in prewar Poland. His words, even in writing, are aglow with truth and beauty.

R. Yehoshua Starrett, a young scholar and devotee of the chasidic tradition, has shown me his English rendition of this diary-journal.

I find R. Starrett's effort superb. He has captured the flavor of the original without sacrificing present English usage. There are many in these troubled times who yearn to still their spiritual thirst through such works as this one. They will be grateful for its appearance.

Rabbi Nachman Bulman
Yeshivat Ohr Somayach
Jerusalem

CONTENTS

CONTENTS

CONTENTS

INTRODUCTION

Holy rebbe, Rebbe Kalonymus Kalman
Shapira o.b.m. of Peasetzna outside Warsaw, in the
pre–World War II chasidic kingdom of Poland. What
can we say about you?

What can we say about a great leader who rather
than escape the horrors of the Holocaust in the hope of
rebuilding elsewhere, chose to go down with his "dear
children"—his students and followers—in the sinking
ship of Polish Jewry, or as more aptly put, to go up in
flames with them? What sense can there be in tending a
dying flock instead of going and starting a new one?
Was this just the ultimate self-sacrifice of a rebbe for
his "children," or was there perhaps more to it?

Looking at the spiritual legacy he left behind, couldn't he have done so much more had he opted to live?

Holy Rebbe Kalonymus Kalman of Peasetzna o.b.m., who can know your real intentions? Yet perhaps we can understand your actions in the context of your teachings.

But first let us see where you came from.

Rebbe Kalonymus was born into an illustrious family of holy rebbes: the Maggid of Kozhnitz (Rebbe Yisrael Hofstein o.b.m.); Rebbe Elimelekh of Lizhensk o.b.m.; the "Seer" of Lublin (Rebbe Ya'akov Yitzchak Horowitz o.b.m.); and the Ma'or Va'Shemesh (Rebbe Kalonymus Kalman Epstein o.b.m., for whom he was named) were among his antecedents. His own father, Rebbe Elimelekh of Grodzisk o.b.m., was very advanced in years when on the 19th of *Iyyar*, 5649 (May 20, 1889), Kalonymus was born.

Young Kalonymus absorbed much from his saintly father, who showed a special affection for him. This was more than just fatherly love—it was out of the great future Rebbe Elimelekh predicted for him. When Kalonymus was only two, his father would put the written petitions (*kvitlakh*) his *chasidim* gave him underneath the sleeping child's pillow. One incident that left such an indelible mark on Kalonymus' sensitive soul that he related it to his close followers decades later happened on *Hoshana Rabbah*—a day Rebbe Elimelekh spent almost entirely in *shul* with his *chasidim* at the sublime and moving *Hoshanot* processions. The young child of two came crying, "Daddy! Daddy!" to his father, who was also crying in prayer. His father answered him, "My son: as you have come crying to me, your father, do you see how I must also cry to God, *my Father?*"

Then, seven weeks before his third birthday, Kalonymus was left an orphan. This scion to and carrier of the rich chasidic tradition would now have to make it on his own.

To be sure, his saintly mother imparted him of her wisdom and character—Rebbe Kalonymus later attested to this after her passing (see "A Memorial Dedication"). She would also take him occasionally to her saintly father, the rebbe of Chentchin, who went out of his way to show his grandson an extra measure of affection and guidance. And on a more steady basis, the older *chasidim* of Grodzisk gave him special attention. Most of all, a much older grandson of Rebbe Elimelekh, a nephew of the young Kalonymus who was himself the Rebbe of Kozhnitz—Rebbe Yerachmiel Moshe—played the major role in educating the child.

Yet, though Kalonymus lost his physical father, his father's spirit and love continued with him. Once, when the orphaned three-year-old was brought into *shul* to recite the *Kaddish*, he looked at his father's empty chair and refused to say it: "How can I recite *Kaddish* when I see my father right there before me?"

So Kalonymus received much love in his formative years: from his father, who due to his age was also like an affectionate great-grandfather; from his widowed but courageous mother; from his maternal grandfather; and from his older nephew, Rebbe Yerachmiel Moshe. It was this love that the Rebbe Kalonymus was later able to pour into whomever came to him for help, whether it was a follower or a stranger.

When Kalonymus was thirteen, Rebbe Yerachmiel Moshe engaged his daughter to his junior uncle. They were married when Kalonymus was sixteen. The following four years Kalonymus spent near his father-in-law, absorbing from him what older, veteran *cha-sidim* hadn't taken in in a lifetime. Rebbe Yerachmiel Moshe was his private tutor and mentor.

Despite all this, the young Kalonymus grew on his own without a physical father. It was perhaps this aloneness in the world that catapulted Kalonymus God-ward. On the other hand, it also allowed him to develop without the constraints of a great father's shadow.

The young Kalonymus was known for his curiosity—fascination—with Creation. He was a musical soul who saw the world as one great harmonic symphony. Perhaps the two go together—at least for Kalonymus they did—and both traits accompanied him throughout life.

His musical talents already appeared in his youth—he was entranced by the "music" of Creation and expressed it both in word and in tune. The works he eventually wrote are not just chasidic classics but are classics of poetic prose.

Even in the simple sense, he was a music composer: he composed original *niggunim* (tunes) for *Shabbat*, *Yom Tov*, and family gatherings. Then, when the *Shabbat* or *Yom Tov* was over, he himself would play the tunes on the fiddle. Those present would sing along with him while he made sure that they did not err even in a single note.

Kalonymus' curiosity eventually led him to acquire knowledge from outside traditional Torah sources. It is known that he read these books in the bathroom. One major subject he studied was medicine to help the ailing. Together with a blessing that he gave to the countless ill who came to him as rebbe, he also gave a pharmaceutical prescription that he wrote in Latin. Expert doctors respected and used his suggestions, though they wondered where such a formally uneducated person got all his knowledge. Almost no Jew underwent surgery in Warsaw without first consulting Rebbe Kalonymus. There were even cases where the doctors feared the operation was too dangerous, but Rebbe Kalonymus took responsibility for it, and it was successful.

Here is a very revealing and instructive anecdote that also shows he knew more than just practical medicine:

The Rebbe used to say that it is not the medicine that heals, but faith in God's loving-kindness. Once, a *chasid* came in to him complaining: "Rebbe! Ever since the medicine got erased from the prescription you wrote, I am suffering again from my headaches." Those followers of the Rebbe present in the room wondered what he meant by "the medicine got erased"—a medicine is either a cream, an ointment, or a liquid. But then, the Rebbe took out a fresh piece of paper and wrote him up once again the prescription. The *chasid* took the piece of paper, picked up his hat, put the prescription in the lining of his undercap, and put both headcoverings back on his head. All of sudden the *chasid* shouted in excitement: "Rebbe! The headache has already subsided! Thank God, I feel again better like before—the letters on this new prescription are clear!"

All the *chasidim* in the room began to chuckle, but the Rebbe explained in all sincerity: "What you have just witnessed is called 'suggestology.' One convinces oneself of a certain thing, such as that a certain medicine will help him, though in truth it is totally ineffective. But we who believe in God as the Creator of all cures can understand this phenomenon very simply—it is our *faith* in God as the Faithful Healer that opens our souls to His healing powers. Nevertheless, I enclothed this abstract medicine in something physical that he could relate to. That's why I wrote out a new prescription. This *chasid* was sure that God's will for him is that his healing come through this written prescription. So as long as the letters on the paper were clear, this supported his faith and his healing. But when the letters became faded, his headache returned, because according to his understanding, he could not receive God's healing. So I rewrote the prescription and he now feels better again. The ultimate healing, though, is when one has absolute faith that God can and will heal him without any physical medicines or doctors."

Young Kalonymus was only twenty when his father-in-law died in 1909, but he was immediately declared rebbe. Peasetzna, the chosen town of this youngest rebbe of the generation, soon became a major center for Polish *chasidim*. The young Rebbe Kalonymus became almost overnight the address for not only broken souls seeking encouragement or help of some sort but also for the elite spiritual seekers searching for guidance to go ever higher—and for everyone in between.

Rebbe Kalonymus spent hours each day lovingly receiving people and listening to each one's story, and this despite his becoming also Rav of Peasetzna in 1913 and personally overseeing the *yeshivah* that he opened in 1923. He used to say, "When someone comes to you for help of some sort, think for a minute before you answer: what would be if the situation were turned around and you were approaching him for help—how would you like *him* to answer?" No wonder people of all sorts were attracted to him—how could they help but love him in return?

One time, several women pushed their way into his room in order to present him with their problems. The Rebbe's attendants began shouting at them. "Is that how you treat distressed women?" the Rebbe answered.

Special interest was given to even the simplest of Jews who came to him for spiritual guidance. They would become his ardent devotees and their lives would be indelibly stamped with his personality. Rebbe Kalonymus became for many the central point of their entire lives and, of course, their Jewishness. One follower once had to travel to another city, and Rebbe Kalonymus asked him to buy him a pipe while he was there. Upon return, the *chasid* reported back to the Rebbe, who then told him: "Do you really think that I needed a pipe? I wanted you to be tied to me in thought even though you were far away."

Most amazing was Rebbe Kalonymus' influence over those Jews estranged from their traditions. Many of them were brought back to the fold after only a single personal meeting with his loving and magnetic personality. They then became his staunch supporters, helping finance his *yeshivah*. Some he even made into pious *chasidim*. Very aptly, Rebbe Kalonymus was called by many great contemporaries "The Spiritual Resurrecter."

After World War I, Rebbe Kalonymus moved his permanent dwelling to Warsaw, though he continued to function as rebbe and rav of Peasetzna, returning there every year from August until after the Sukkot festival. In Warsaw he was confronted with the Sabbath desecration epidemic of the 1920s by the irreligious Jewish socialists. In this, too, Rebbe Kalonymus accomplished with his love and understanding what others were unable to do with their campaigning.

He used to say that in every single Jew, even in the most belligerently antireligious, is a spark of the Jewish soul that needs only to be reached, opened, and ignited in the right way. Rebbe Kalonymus knew how to do this. After several meetings with him, these hard socialist leaders admitted their difficulty arguing with him and said wryly: "We'd rather have the aggressive tactics of others than the love, patience, and humility of Rebbe Kalonymus."

Rebbe Kalonymus was indeed a most devoted

leader, both in the spiritual and the material sense. "A rebbe who is not willing to enter the *Gehinnom* to save a follower is not a rebbe!" he used to say. And he was willing to give away the shirt on his back to help the simplest of people.

Despite his abounding love for all Jewish people, his love for children and youngsters was even greater. *They* were the future of the Jewish People. They were the ones whom he insisted surround him at the *Shabbat* morning services with their loud prayers. They were the ones for whom he opened a *yeshivah* in 1923 in order to train a generation of future leaders.

"The entire burden of being rebbe I bear only in order to be able to support the *yeshivah*, and the entire burden of the *yeshivah* I bear in order to produce ten spiritual giants who will be the future leaders," is what he used to say. And he meant it literally: nearly every penny that people donated when they came to him for his help he passed on to the *yeshivah* that same day. That sometimes came to a nice amount. And this despite the privation and debt for the *yeshivah* that he personally lived in.

In addition to running the *yeshivah*, Rebbe Kalonymus also led a private group of elite spiritual seekers for whom he composed a small but potent guidebook that he instructed not be shown to outsiders. We can understand the Rebbe's desire for secrecy as the need of these deep searchers for growth in privacy without the impediment of social sanction. In that booklet and in our journal, the Rebbe bemoans the detrimental effects of being socially conscious. Of course, this group was not meant to be monastic but to spread its influence whether by intermind thought flows, as the Rebbe mentions in the journal, or by their intermingling with society. It was meant to be a core group of high spiritual energy.

But Rebbe Kalonymus did not ignore the average or weak student: "Each and every one is as dear and beloved to me as my own child," he would say. Each student received the Rebbe's personal attention and any ailing one was brought to the Rebbe's home until recuperated.

It was to these students of his *yeshivah*, the youths for whom he wanted to create a brighter future, that he would always say: "My dearest children . . . the *most important thing in the world* . . . is to do someone else a favor. . . ." Rebbe Kalonymus sought to pass on his boundless love to the future. He himself never had more than two childless children.

Rebbe Kalonymus' success with his *yeshivah* was not due only to his own brilliant lectures, nor even only to the endless love he gave to each student. Rebbe Kalonymus was a pedagogue par excellence and a master psychologist of the student's soul. He would interview each student at length until he reached the core of his soul and then be able to guide him on his individual path. He was able to, figuratively speaking, extract the student's soul, to shine it, uplift it, and remold it, performing a "heart and mind surgery" to transform the person.

Somehow, despite his heavy schedule, Rebbe Kalonymus found time to write. *Chovat HaTalmidim*, the only book of his that was printed in his lifetime, became a classic as soon as it came out in 1932, and not only in chasidic Poland of the 1930s but also in Israel and England decades later. The head of a nonchasidic Jerusalem *yeshivah* asked the Rebbe's heirs to reprint it without the last three explicitly chasidic essays. They refused. But this shows how accepted and sought after is the Rebbe's pedagogy even outside chasidic circles.

Another curious anecdote is that of the head of a nonchasidic *yeshivah* in England who banned the book from the *yeshivah*'s library, fearing its chasidic influence on the students. The local Jewish bookstore owner said that there was never such a run on his bookstore to buy copies.

Even beyond religious circles, the Rebbe's pedagogy was recognized and lauded. A former mayor of Haifa, Mr. Aryeh Gur'el, who learned in his youth at the Rebbe's *yeshivah*, attests to having shown the Rebbe's books to secular educationalists who were highly impressed with his methods. Rebbe Kalonymus rightly deserved the title given him in prewar Poland, the "Pedagogic Rebbe."

The 1930s were the height of Rebbe Kalonymus' prewar greatness. One well-known chasidic journalist of the time wrote after the war that he personally knew the more than three hundred chasidic rebbes of Poland and the surroundings. Each one, he wrote, was great in something different: this one in breadth of Torah knowledge and that one in depth; this one in love of the Jewish People and that one in prayer devotions; this one in this trait and that one in another. But the Rebbe of Peasetzna, he said, was great in *all of them*.

And then World War II broke out. Even before Poland collapsed two weeks later, the Rebbe's daughter-in-law and wife's sister were killed by the bombing, and his only son lay dying of wounds. Then his son died, and two weeks later his elderly mother died of anguish. Now, except for a married daughter, Rebbe Kalonymus was alone. (His wife had died two years earlier.)

Whatever inner greatness Rebbe Kalonymus had managed to conceal until then, now his soul on fire became fully revealed. Now he could devote all his love to his People—Jewish survival was now the only thing on his mind.

Whether it was consoling the bereaved or encouraging the broken, Rebbe Kalonymus was there even more than before. Whether it was somehow corresponding with followers who had escaped to Japan or keeping open the free kitchen in his home for the homeless, Rebbe Kalonymus did it all. Whether it was maintaining his *yeshivah* as long as feasible or holding a *Shalosh Seudos* lecture when there was nothing to eat, Rebbe Kalonymus rose to the call. Whether it was endangering his own life to save a youth from the Gestapo or searching for the whereabouts of someone in need of funds—both while his own son lay dying— Rebbe Kalonymus had the inner strength. Whether it was maintaining the *Yom Tov* spirit as his son lay dying or singing on Simchat Torah days after he died or even spreading joy on Purim in 1941 (!!!), Rebbe Kalonymus had it in him. Even in the forced labor factory, he continued to be a center of Jewish life. And until the liquidation of the Warsaw Ghetto in the spring of 1943, Rebbe Kalonymus remained with his People, then going with those remaining to Treblinka. There, on the 4th of *Cheshvan*, 5704 (November 2, 1943), his soul went up in fire to Heaven.

What inner drive drew Rebbe Kalonymus into the Warsaw Ghetto at the outbreak of war and kept him there despite offers of escape? Was it out of the same sense of mission that already in the 1920s had moved him to commit his spiritual journal to posterity and moved him to personally write his ghetto lectures? Perhaps we can explain it with a very pregnant statement he once made.

At one point in the ghetto, Rebbe Kalonymus con-

tracted typhus and became seriously ill for several
months. Medically speaking, there was no way for him
to survive. Once, word went around that he had died.
Thousands flocked to his house despite the danger
involved. The Rebbe became aware of the crowd gath-
ered outside. With the greatest of effort, he overcame
his weakness and said: "*Gevalt*! How tragic and pitiful!
You have come to cry over me, but I feel like crying
over the entire Jewish People."

We are taught that when one cries at the funeral of
a great person, he becomes able to draw from the
essence of that person's soul. This is because each soul
has a unique channel for receiving godliness, but when
one dies, that channel is closed up. When another Jew
cries over the loss of this great man and feels the
vacuum created by his death, then the inner hole thus
made in that person's soul becomes a new outlet for
that old channel. It is as if the affinity between the two
souls draws back the essence of the deceased soul into
this world.

Rebbe Kalonymus said that there are sources of
spiritual energy that can be tapped into only when one
really feels their lack. The more you feel their lack, the
more you feel that you *must* have them. But once one
person has brought them into this world, they are in
circulation for others to receive also.

So Rebbe Kalonymus was crying over the Jewish
People, an entire people that was dying out. What could
he do to save his People but become an embodiment of
all that they were? He would become the channel to
transmit teachings that were at the essence of the Jewish
soul. Of all the Jewish leaders of that time, his were the
only manuscripts to be found after the war. He had a
message for all future generations, a message that could
not be lost. He went up in flames with the Jewish

People, and because he so mourned their lack, he was able to draw them back into the world with new spiritual dimensions.

Holy Rebbe Kalonymus, what more can we say? Can we at least say that we follow your teachings? You cried over the Jewish People during the war—where are we, the Jewish People today? Where are the true chasidim, *the type you wanted to make: lovers of God, of fellow Jews, and of all Creation? Where are all the spiritual seekers who so followed you—did they all go up in flames together with you?*

We have been so busy since the war rebuilding the Jewish edifice: we have built many yeshivot *and filled them with students and books, but you ask us, have we filled them with God also?*

What can we answer, holy Rebbe Kalonymus? You have already answered this, as well.

We shall study your works, your spiritual classics. We shall practice them in our lives. We shall yearn for a rebbe who could personally guide us through the pitfalls of the spiritual life. We shall feel the deep pain of lacking such a mentor. We shall feel the loss of your guidance in our lives.

And may this vacuum that we feel at the core of our souls reopen the channels of your soul. May your soul then, in some hidden way, come to guide us and enlighten this dark night of our souls.

Translating Rebbe Kalonymus' journal and then studying his life in order to write this introduction has been for me a very uplifting experience. I hope that it will be also for all those who read it. I feel deeply grateful to have had the privilege of working on this and of presenting it to the public.

Rebbe Kalonymus' works are unique among chasidic literature. By and large, the latter are all "insider's stories," taking the initiated reader to beautiful places. They assume prior knowledge of the reader and training in chasidic practice and thought. Without that, the reader can at most get only an intellectual grasp of the subject matter, but the doors of experience remain closed. Many of them speak in abstruse parlance, concealing more than they convey. Mystic messages are muffled and camouflaged behind the facade of a Torah commentary. If a reader does not already have the chasidic mind-set and Torah thought, he will most likely miss the message.

Rebbe Kalonymus' books are different—not only because of their poetic style but also because of their pedagogic genius. In lucid language and descriptive detail, Rebbe Kalonymus speaks to the reader's soul. With few quotations, with no obscure allusions, without awkward Torah interpretations, before us are opened the doors to a new world. Literally taking us by the hand, Rebbe Kalonymus leads us into the chasidic world.

This in no way is meant to detract from the greatness of other chasidic works. Each one is meant for a different audience and some even for different periods of time. Perhaps due to antichasidic pressures, these other works had to be written in cryptic ways. And perhaps they were written only for followers, who were already privy to this way.

As Rebbe Kalonymus himself writes in his *M'vo HaShearim* (*An Introduction to the Gates [of Chasidut]*, chap. 1), each new Torah revelation is a prophetic spirit of sorts, and each prophet speaks in a unique way. The prophet Yeshaya definitely saw "more" than the prophet Yechezkel, but the latter spoke in a more vivid way. And it is also a need of the generation: today we need more explicit ways.

So in poetic language, Rebbe Kalonymus takes us on a journey to the above and beyond. He uplifts us above the mundane hubbub and brings us into the chasidic world. He teaches us specific techniques to guide us along our way. He brings us to feel that *we ourselves are holy* and not only the holy books that we learn.

Rebbe Kalonymus himself marveled at the beauty of his book *Chovat HaTalmidim*. In reference to it he said: "If I myself did not know that I had authored it, I would never be able to believe that I could. It was really only the Hand of God writing through me."

Unique even among Rebbe Kalonymus' works is this one, his journal: in it he gives us a glimpse into his personal spiritual world. This does not mean that his other books do not; the music in the words, the deep insights, the crystal-clear diction, the message of great import he so potently conveys, and of course, the loving guidance all give us a picture of how rich was his inner life. But only in this one, his journal, does he speak so intimately and directly about himself.

Although Rebbe Kalonymus himself referred to this work in a letter as just a pamphlet of brief essays, he wrote in a different letter circa 1928 that he had begun keeping a journal of concise admonitions titled *An Exhortation and Behest*. This title must have taken on for Rebbe Kalonymus solemn and supreme added meaning at a much later date. That was in 1943 under the conditions of the war, when Jewish survival was so uncertain. Rebbe Kalonymus lovingly, defiantly, and tenaciously, though perhaps tearfully, placed his manuscripts in a tin container and buried it underneath the Warsaw Ghetto deep in the ground. In the attached letter, he again referred to this work as *An Exhortation and Behest*. But now it was also to mean his last spiritual will and testament to whatever Jews might be left—by then he himself was wifeless and without children.

Nevertheless, because of the very nature and style of the book, I have taken the liberty to title it simply as his journal. Besides, what greater spiritual will and testament could Rebbe Kalonymus leave us with other than his personal spiritual journal? This, indeed, is what he himself says in the very first entry: "Bequeathing a Spiritual Journal to Posterity." Though the actual entry titles are not part of the manuscript but are mine, in this opening passage Rebbe Kalonymus seems to be prophetically telling us why he really wrote this book.

Since the essence of the book was meant to be its timeless message and not a message about the times, Rebbe Kalonymus did not date the entries. Several, though, can be dated: after beginning the journal circa 1928, as mentioned in the above cited letter and verified by his followers, in 19 the Rebbe states he is past thirty-nine but not yet forty. That means it was somewhere between spring 1928 and spring 1929. Then 25 has a footnote that seems to show it was also written around that time; 26 can also perhaps be dated as 1929 because of an almost identical theme in 47 from the Rebbe's other journal, which was written before 48 and which *is* dated fall 1929. 27 is the Rebbe's account of his famous somersaulting, which he did on Shavuot, or early summer, of 1929. This means that most of the journal is from 1928 to 1929, as borne out by his followers.

Then in 30 there is a jump to late 1932, and 35 is probably from early 1935 with a postscript from late 1939. With that last tearful but prayerful note after the tragic death of his son, the Rebbe closed this book.

Though Rebbe Kalonymus kept this journal for

posterity and expressly willed its publication, he did not censor any self-demeaning statements. On the contrary. We are in fact awed, almost bewildered, by this holy man's mid-life confessions (19). At the same time, we dare not take him literally by our standards; he judged himself according to his own. For him, to lose consciousness of God or to slacken in his intense devotions must have been deplorable. Hence the severe self-censure.

One glaring question we are faced with in this book is the Rebbe's seeming outburst of disdain, almost vexation, at materialistic and unspiritual people (34). Considering Rebbe Kalonymus' boundless love even for the most defiantly estranged Jew, as mentioned before, where did this emotion come from?

Perhaps we can understand it as follows:

In 48, the Rebbe states explicitly something that is implicit throughout his entire life and works: a passion to bring the world closer to God. But people in general were not responding to his call. So Rebbe Kalonymus admits that he became upset and depressed—as he says will happen when aspirations remain unrealized (23).

But depression can hide buried frustration. Perhaps Rebbe Kalonymus was vexed by people not as passionate as he. So we can accept this one known outburst as an expression of his frustrated burning desire.

The Rebbe's outcries against the anti-Semitic nations (30) can be understood as a response to persecution. But Rebbe Kalonymus transcended this anger, as we find no evidence of it in his Ghetto-time Torah lectures. After losing his only son and daughter-in-law to Nazi bombing, after seeing Jews mass-murdered by the Nazi beasts, Rebbe Kalonymus has no harsh words for them—he accepts suffering yet prays for relief. Perhaps it was the awesome angst he endured both for his personal and for Jewish affliction that actually lifted him above it.

The deep psychological insights and specific, almost Eastern-style, meditation techniques that we find in this journal make us wonder whether they were oral tradition, the Rebbe's own findings, or if he learned them in his "reading room." We cannot know for sure, but it does not really matter. The very fact that Rebbe Kalonymus incorporated them into his spiritual life and presents them to us for posterity is enough sanction that they are "Jewish." In Appendix A, I have translated an excerpt from his *Hakhsharat HaAvrekhim* where he speaks about contemporary secular psychology. It is obvious that he knew at least something about it.

The two pairs of entries that are almost identical (15 and 38, 16 and 41) are due to the two separate journals included in this book. But since there are slight changes, I have translated them slightly differently to give each a unique flavor. And to make the reading of certain portions easier and more potent, I have entered the Rebbe's dialogue with God or with "people" in quotation marks. All source notes are my addition.

I take this opportunity to thank my friend and associate Ozer Bergman, the editor of a previous work of mine, for reviewing the translated manuscript and offering his suggestions. Many of them have been incorporated into the text.

I offer my deep appreciation to my mother, Mrs. Jacqueline Starrett, for typing this manuscript and to my father, Mr. Louis Starrett, for his technical help.

I am much obliged to Rabbi Menachem Shapira of Bnei Brak, a grandnephew of Rebbe Kalonymus and acting heir for printing the Rebbe's books. He graciously gave me permission to do this translation and spent much time on the phone with me answering questions regarding the book. I also thank Mr. Nesan'el Radziner, a follower of Rebbe Kalonymus, and Mr. Chaim Frenkel for their help. A tithe of my earnings from this book will go toward a fund dedicated to proliferating the Rebbe's books.

And my deep gratitude goes to Mr. Arthur Kurzweil of Jason Aronson Inc. for his wisdom in seeing the need for a translation of this book and for giving me the privilege to do it.

As a fitting close to this introduction and simultaneously a proper preface, even preamble, to this book, I offer the following translation of an essay written by a student of the Rebbe. I suggest that the reader refer to it frequently. I also suggest that no more than one entry be read at a time, and reread for meditation.

Inner Silence

In 5696 or 5697 (1935 or 1936), the period during which I studied together with____ , we merited to be called in to the Rebbe between Rosh Hashanah and Yom Kippur. It was probably in my friend's merit: the Rebbe seemed to be very happy with our learning together, so when the Rebbe would call him in, I was called in also. It was at this occasion that I first heard about the practice of inner silence. Unfortunately, I do not remember the entire discussion, but I shall write down what I do remember for posterity.

The Rebbe began by mentioning the saying of our Sages that a dream is a sixtieth of prophecy (*Berakhot* 57b). As is known, the Rebbe's approach throughout his works is that a person's selfness is what prevents divine inspiration. Therefore, when a person is *self*-conscious and his ego thoughts are flowing, it is unlikely that he will receive any inspiration. But when a person is asleep and his ego thoughts are silenced, he may then specifically receive inspiration because his conscious ego is now out of action. This is how he explained why a dream is a sixtieth of prophecy.

The Rebbe's saying on why people become more inspired during prayer than during Torah learning is also known. During Torah learning, our ego-selves are more active: our underlying feeling is that "I am learning" or that "I think such and such." But the essence of prayer is the very opposite: a surrender of our ego-selves.

The point is, though, that when a person is asleep he cannot will or aspire to anything—he is asleep. So the goal must be to come to a state of "sleep" even while awake, that is to still the mind of its incessant flow of thoughts and desires. This is because by nature, human thoughts are so enmeshed with one another that it is difficult to let go of them. (As I once heard from the Rebbe, if a person would pay attention to his incessant thought flow even for just one day, he would see that there is almost no difference between his own and the psychotic's thought flow. Besides the fact that the psychotic acts out his thoughts, the thoughts themselves of the normal, average person are the same as the psychotic's thoughts.) The Rebbe then gave us practical techniques to silence the mind.

He said that one should begin by observing his thoughts for a short while, even if only for a few minutes: "What am I thinking about now?" Slowly he will begin to feel his mind emptying out and his thoughts coming to rest from their usual flow. Then one should begin to recite a verse such as, "God, the Ultimate Truth," in order to bind his mind, now emptied of other thoughts, to a single holy thought. Afterward, one will be able to elicit God's help for spiritual advancement, such as strengthening one's faith or one's love and awe of God. I then merited to witness the Rebbe actually meditate for strengthening faith. He said, "I believe with unwavering faith that the Creator is the only single Being in existence. There is no true existence besides Him. All of Creation and all that is in it is nothing but a ray of Divine Light." He repeated this several times. Such meditations should not be said forcefully; the goal is to keep the mind quiet from the flow of thoughts, and forceful repetition will only rearouse the ego. Repeat the meditations very softly.

I also merited to hear the Rebbe meditate for love of God. He said, "I want very much to be close to God. I want very much to feel close to the great Creator." He also said at this occasion that such meditation can be used for all types of character improvement. The repetitions should not be phrased in the negative but in the positive, desired opposite of the specific unwanted trait. For example, someone who is lackadaisical would not phrase his repetitions that he stop being lazy but rather that he become industrious and energetic. He explained this with an example from real life: if a child is crying, the more we tell him to stop crying, the more he will cry.

Another technique he gave us to quiet the mind is to focus on the small hand of a clock, which barely moves as you watch it. This also tends to silence a person's thoughts and desires.

After we reached the state of inner silence, so conducive of divine inspiration, he directed us to repeat with him the verse, "Guide me, God, along Your pathways" (Psalm 27:11), with the special tune he always used. How pleasant and awesome was this experience that I merited only on my friend's account.

The Rebbe spoke at length about this subject, saying how sure he was of its potent effectiveness. He said that after a few weeks of faith repetitions in the inner-silence state, when one recites the verse, "This is my God and I shall adorn Him" (Exodus 15:2), one will be able to "point with his finger," as it says in the *Midrash* (*Exodus Rabbah* 23:15), that is, he will have an immediate experience of the divine.

At this first occasion, we did not merit to fully grasp the Rebbe's teaching. It was only some time later that we merited again to hear from him about this in greater detail. He strongly urged us to keep this practice.

May God grant us all the inner silence and inner peace that the Rebbe is here trying to convey. Amen.

THE JOURNAL

ATTENTION!!!

I take the privilege of allowing myself to ask of the honorable person or institution that will find my enclosed manuscripts—*A Preliminary Guide for Mature Students*, *An Introduction to the Gates [of Chasidut]*, a part of *The Work of Mature Students*, *[A Journal of]Exhortation and Behest*, and *Torah Lectures* on the weekly portions from 5700, 5701, and 5702 [1940 to 1942]—to be as kind as to send them to the Land of Israel to the following address: "Rabbi Yeshayah Shapira, Tel Aviv, Palestine," together with the following letter. If God will show mercy and I remain alive with other Jews after the war, I hereby request to return all of these papers to the Warsaw Rabbinate for Kalonymus. May God have mercy on us, the remnant of the Jewish People wherever we are, rescue us, keep us alive, and save us promptly.

With heartfelt gratitude,
Kalonymus

Sunday evening, week of *VaAyra Tevet* 26, 5703 [January 3, 1943]

To the honorable Rabbi Yeshayah Shapira, long life to him.

To my illustrious friend R' Avner Binenthal; to my faithful friend R'Elimelekh ben Porat; and to my beloved brothers and friends who are so near to my heart, long life to them all.

The work *A Preliminary Guide for Mature Students* was already being printed before the war but this was interrupted when war broke out. Now we are in perilous danger every day, God forbid. So I ask of you, my beloved friends: when, with God's help, you receive the manuscripts *A Preliminary Guide for Mature Students*, *An Introduction to the Gates [of Chasidut]* (from *The Work of Mature Students*), *[A Journal of] Exhortation and Behest*, and *Torah Lectures* from the brutal years 5700 to 5702, please see to have them printed either together or separately, however you see fit. Please also see to distribute them in Jewish circles. I also request that you print on each edition that I personally request and beseech of each and every Jew to learn my works. The merit of my holy ancestors o.b.m. will assuredly stand by him and all his family in this world and the next. May God have mercy on us.

At the beginning of the *Preliminary Guide* that was then being printed, I placed only a memorial page for my saintly wife o.b.m. Then things were still good for me: my saintly mother o.b.m., my martyred son, and martyred daughter-in-law were still alive. But now, to my deep grief and anguish, I have lost all these treasures—the light of my life has been doused. So I ask to print the following memorials, which I shall write down.

May God have mercy and say "Enough!" to the affliction of the Jewish People and to my personal torment. May He return to me my dear, sweet, and modest daughter Rekhil Yehudit, long life to her, who was kidnapped from me on the second day of *Rosh Chodesh Elul*, Friday in the week of *Shoftim* 5702 [August 14, 1942].

Also please print on the title page of the above books my name together with those of my holy father o.b.m. and holy father-in-law o.b.m.

I cannot write anymore. May God have mercy and keep us alive with the rest of the remaining Jews so that I myself may merit to have them printed.

Your beloved brother and friend who yearns for you, broken and crushed from my torture and that of the Jewish People, which is deep as the greatest depths and high as the highest heavens, I am, awaiting God's immediate salvation,

Kalonymus

A MEMORIAL DEDICATION

In eternal memory of my saintly mother and mentor, the righteous and valiant woman of noble descent, Mrs. Chanah Brocho o.b.m., daughter of the saintly and holy Rebbe Chaim Shmuel HaLevi o.b.m. of Chentchin. She served God with all her might, with heart and soul, and raised her children to a Torah life with painstaking effort. Her holy soul rose up in purity to Heaven on the eve of *Erev Shabbat*, the 7th of *Cheshvan*, 5700 [October 20, 1939].

And of my righteous, modest, and pious wife of noble descent, Mrs. Rachel Chayah Miriam o.b.m., daughter of the righteous and holy Rebbe Yerachmiel Moshe o.b.m., rabbi of Kozhnitz. Her virtues were superlative, and she learned Torah every day. She was like a compassionate mother to souls in general and especially to Torah students and *chasidim*. Her holy soul rose up in purity to Heaven during the prime of her life on the holy *Shabbat*, the weekly portion of "And Miriam died there (*Chukat*)," the 10th of *Tammuz*, 5697 [June 19, 1937].

And of my only son, the joy of my heart and soul, the holy scholar and *chasid* of noble descent, Rabbi Elimelekh Ben-Tzion o.b.m., a man of truth, of refined character traits, a profound Torah scholar and sage, and lover of the Jewish People. He left behind Torah novellas on the tractate *Shabbat* and on the first part of *Yoreh De'ah*.

He was mortally wounded during the dire times for our People on Monday the 12th of *Tishrei* 5700 [September 25, 1939]. After great and bitter suffering he returned his holy soul to Heaven on the 16th of *Tishrei*, the second day of Sukkot [September 29, 1939].

And of his wife, my holy daughter-in-law, refined and modest, of noble descent, Mrs. Gittel o.b.m., daughter of the righteous Rebbe Shlomo Chaim, long may he live [o.b.m.], of Balkhav. While in danger to her own life, she stood outside the hospital where her husband, my holy son o.b.m. lay wounded. She was killed on Tuesday, the 13th of *Tishrei* of the aforementioned year.

May the Source of all mercy hold them close under His wings for all eternity and bind their souls to the Source of Life. God is their inheritance. May they rest in peace. Amen.

1

BEQUEATHING A SPIRITUAL
JOURNAL TO POSTERITY

How rewarding it would be if after the end of our lives, we could live another seventy years. We struggle a lifetime training ourselves to uncover our self-deceptions and to nurture the inner greatness of our souls. Then, in a second lifetime, we could reap the fulfillment of living a perfected life even in this imperfect world. But suddenly, after decades of struggle, instead we are gone . . . taken back into the womb of God.

This being the case, the second best thing is to record your inner life in a journal. This will not be something you do to earn immortal fame as an author, but rather to engrave your soul-portrait on paper. Write down all your inner struggles, your setbacks and successes, and grant them eternal life. This way your very essence, the personality of your soul, your spiritual attainments, your life's inner treasures, will live on forever in the lives of your spiritual heirs as generations come and go.[1]

---

[1]When readers incorporate an author's essence into their own lives by following his teachings, living his lessons, and passing them on to the next generation, then the author's very soul lives on for eternity in the lives of those who bear his essence. The author's soul thus dons a different mode of expression as the generations come and go.

2

WHO DO YOU WANT TO BE?

If your life's aim is to serve God with constant improvement and to reach age seventy beyond your *bar mitzvah* level, then here is the thing to do:

Each year, clarify a goal and envision the actualized "you" of next year. Visualize who this "you" will be: his attainments . . . his daily life . . . his character . . . and his inner essence. Use this envisioned "you" also as a gauge to know how far you still have to go. Is your present daily progress enough to create the reality of that envisioned future "you"?

But if next year comes and you have not actualized that "you," it is as if your life has been cut short. The new "you" was aborted, it is not alive now, you are still an old "you" of perhaps years ago.

This is the meaning of "And Avraham was old, advanced in years" (Genesis 24:1): the Avraham of this year was the advanced Avraham of this year, not the Avraham of the past.

3

PASSING OPPORTUNITIES
FOR GROWTH

W hen your conceit is at wane, when your boldness is low, when your ego defenses are down—do not yet think you have "made it." Rather, move fast to go deep inside, grab the chance to work on yourself. Plow through your hardened inner blocks, heal the wounds of your soul. With honest soul-searching, without self-deception, clean out all the poison from your soul.

But quickly! Because even though now you feel a surrender to God, you may only be responding to an unfulfilled wish. Maybe it's sadness over an unreceived honor, or some other frustrated wish turns you to God, although you yourself are unaware of it all. You cannot be sure that the minute your wish is fulfilled, your broken heart will not reossify. An iron curtain will close off the temporary breach, your heart itself will feel like stone. Sealed and boarded up at every possible entrance, you remain locked outside yourself.

You now may long to heal the wounds of your soul, but alas, how can you when you are outside?

4

SOUL-HEALING

Imagine how you would look if you had fulfilled your every wish—every thought, desire, and fancy you ever had in your life. How immoral and depraved you would be!

So how fortunate you are that you yourself do not look that way, but only because you have ignored those inner voices and not expressed them in real life. Are you then inherently better than the jailed criminal who now cannot commit a crime? Chains and guards and the locks on his prison cell door may keep him in place, but look well into yourself: are you truly not just the same? Would not that "criminal" part of yourself break the bonds of its inner prison if only it could in order to fulfill its heart's desires?

And even if you have taken such control of your mind that any intruding thought you immediately cast aside, congratulations!—but don't be complacent with this. Rather, listen to this advice: heal your soul at its source and don't just rely on self-control.

Healing versus Symptomatic Treatment

An analogy would be someone with a gastric infection that causes him to regurgitate. If he visits a quack doctor who treats only the symptoms, the infection itself will not be healed. The infection will continue to spread, pus and poisoned blood will increase. The underlying causes will overcome the suppressing drug, and the patient will again regurgitate. And now it will be more difficult to heal the wound. But if instead he visits a true healer whose wisdom can get to the cause, then with God's help, this doctor will find and heal the infection at its source.

Similarly, there are people who are hounded by untoward thoughts, desires, and tendencies both during waking hours and in their dreams—even those thoughts that they would not consciously allow themselves find entry at unconscious times. In fact, several elderly people have bemoaned to me that even for things that they cannot anymore physically do, nevertheless, as if to spite, these thoughts still hound them. Some of these stories are so shockingly shameful, I would not quote them here in my journal. Here is a milder one:

What Can Happen in Old Age

An elderly peasant came to me crying and screaming—he has a weak heart, but that was not his complaint. Rather, whenever he gets palpitations, he gets a thought to cross himself and be healed. So compulsive becomes this thought that he can barely restrain himself.

I questioned these unfortunate souls and delved into their distant past: I found no wanton lives, contrary to what even they thought of themselves. Even now, they abhor these thoughts. However, their entire lives they worked only on their conscious thoughts and emotions to prevent their baser desires from taking control of them. Their very souls, though, they did not heal. So they were successful in that their infected souls did not spew up their desires into their minds and hearts, but this infection continued to fester inside. Now when they are old and weak and have difficulty controlling themselves, the inborn drives of their souls explode into their thoughts and emotions.

This is what happened to that old peasant. In his youth, he had heard of many bluff miracle healings from gentile peasants. Even though he would never convert, nevertheless these stories resonated in his ignorant and simple soul. He was able to keep them out of his conscious mind and emotions, but they had affected—infected—the depths of his unconscious soul. Now in his old age, these phantoms are coming to haunt him. All the much more so with other old people whose present compulsive thoughts are natural human desires.

These elderly people now see themselves as great sinners and as having forfeited their entire Jewishness. In torment, they now say: "My entire life I knew that my days were numbered and that I am constantly nearing my end. Nevertheless, my consolation was that as I age, my baser desires will also wane with my strength. I looked forward to becoming refined and purified and constantly coming close to God. What I was unable to do in my youth, I'd be able to accomplish in old age. But now—what has become of me? My mind and inner world have become a den for beastly thoughts and a home for the underworld! I am terrified of and shudder at these filthy thoughts that roam in my mind and prey at my heart! Who can vouch that these very thoughts will not greet me as my life flickers out, and to them in my last minutes will I hand over my soul?''

One of these gentlemen was so embittered with life that he said: "I'd rather die than continue living such a despicable life! Is this how I shall get close to God? How shall I return my soul to my Creator? With what disgrace will I have to face God?''

Will It Happen to You?

Now even though this does not happen to every aging person, would you ignore watching your physical health just because only a minority of people get ill? How can you be sure it will not happen to you if you do not take care of yourself? Each of us is responsible for healing the dysfunction of his own soul, the root source of his disturbing thoughts, and not just for keeping them out of his mind and heart.

Do not be startled at what may seem an unreasonable demand to uproot all untoward desire from your soul. Yes, this level was reached by King David, who neutralized his inner evil, but that is not what I ask of you. Far be it from me to demand such exalted levels, and if you think I have, you have misunderstood my request. What I ask of you are levels you can, please God, reach.

Take One Step at a Time

Let us return to the analogy of gastric infection. The quack is satisfied to suppress the symptoms, while the healer aims to heal the wound. There is no assurance, though, that a new infection will never arise. Still, the present wound can be thoroughly healed and the infection expelled. This is the difference. King David so completely neutralized his inner evil at its source that he was sure he would never again be tempted from within to any sort of inappropriate behavior. What I ask of you is that at this moment when that untoward thought, desire, or emotion rises to your consciousness that you not just deflect it and suppress it to your subconscious. Do not celebrate victory over your symptoms—your inner dynamics have not changed. You've just covered your mouth so that your spew remains inside. Heal your soul deep inside where the infection is. Even though another thought or desire may arise again, each time one does, deal with it then and there.

The Essential Factor for Success

But how do we heal the soul? The truth is, it is a long learning process, and several different methods are necessary to know. May God grant me to expound more upon this elsewhere. For now, let us say that the preliminary to all solutions and basis of all consequent techniques is: take responsibility for yourself to find your own personalized solution.

The reason for this can be compared to someone who habitually relies on others financially. Eventually he becomes so lackadaisical and unmotivated that he can hardly be bothered to make good use of his stipend to provide for himself. He will only become mature enough to stand on his own two feet when he realizes that the battle of life is fought within his soul and that it is his own responsibility to wage this war for himself and for those dependent upon him as well. Advice and commands from superiors are insufficient: you must devise original plans for yourself. Outside sources can only be a guideline.

The path outlined by our holy Sages of all generations is not to be strayed from, but within it you must carve your own way. Apply their general rules to your personal situation to solve the problems of your own spiritual life. Only then are you prepared to fight the inner battle, because only then can you make use of the potent words of the wise. Abstract knowledge unpersonalized for your life only leaves you like a soldier without ammunition.

Talking It Out

Besides your many plans of action that you should use until you have healed your soul, you can also take advantage of our Sages' advice based on the verse in Proverbs 12:25: "When a person has a heavy heart, let him speak it out to others" (*Yoma* 75a). The Sages make no mention of what the listener should do to ease the distress of the other. That's because just talking about it and getting it out in the open are so healing and prevent the need for self-deception to numb the buried pain. The Baal Shem Tov explained the verse "My soul was brought out when it [the soul] spoke" (Song of Songs 5:6) in this context. You can experience this with your own anger or upset: you may feel that the emotional pain has subsided, but it's only from your conscious world. Inside, the poisonous emotions still hide. If more events continue to evoke those same emotions and you continue to suppress them out of "sight," eventually your emotional bank will be bursting and will explode when even slightly provoked.

This is the reason depressive people become depressed at the drop of a hat. There is no evident cause for their mood swing beyond the evocation of buried pain by associated ideas. This would not happen if they had a trusted friend before whom they could pour out their hearts. They would immediately feel a load off their hearts and the pain lifted from their souls.

This is the point: do you have a more intimate ally and trusted confidant than your always-there-for-you Father in Heaven?

Cathartic Prayer

So seclude yourself in a quiet place, get as far as you can from distraction. [Relax any tension in your body; quiet all noise in your mind.] Then, envision yourself standing before God: there you are, mortal creature, beseeching the Infinite One. Pour out your heart, speak out your soul, tell Him what's on your mind. Without inhibitions, in whatever language, say whatever comes to your mind.

If you have never before practiced such intimate expression before God, I will give you an example. The goal is to empty out your soul in meditative prayer and return it to its Father's love. This must come from your own heart, so my words are only a guideline:

"God! From the depths of my soul I call out to You, Creator of my very existence. My body, my spirits, and my soul, they are Yours—I have no intrinsic existence. My yearning is great, can't You see, to be pure of spirit and heart. Oh, that Your will would I sense, Your wisdom would I ponder, and Your voice would I hear in my heart. But alas, this is not; my heart mourns inside that my soul is so muddled and confused. I sense only the sensual and desire the impure, and my inner voice no longer transmits Your will. Instead, there inside is the voice of my own will to whose demands I am at beck and call. And even when I try to rise in protest, to expel all that unwanted will, I only can clean out my conscious thoughts—the unconscious remain in my soul.

"God, Pure One and Source of all Purity, how I just fall apart by the thought: if one wishes to clean his house and his garden, he will remove all unwanted things, but when I clean out myself so that my soul shines before You, I just place my waste out of my sight—deep inside my soul where my conscious mind cannot see it. I feel so filthy because of this sewage that putrefies in the depths of my soul. My soul bursts at the seams because of this load that floods forth at most inopportune times. Even now, God, as I speak to You, thoughts of . . . [specify] are knocking at my mind. It is only with Your help that I can restrain the urge to act out these inner voices. But how bitter I feel that my soul is so soiled by those drives that express themselves in various ways in my life.

"Please, God, have mercy and purify my soul; root out those weeds from my soul. Remove all these urges that make me stray from You so that they do not come to haunt me in old age. Especially when I feel intimate with You, when learning Your Torah or when talking to You, let my soul rise right up before You, purified by having fulfilled Your will. Let my soul soar fueled by my yearning to surrender completely to You."

5

SINNING AGAINST YOURSELF

o not underestimate the gravity of an act that hurts no one else but you. Do not say, "I have not sinned, or even overindulged in innocent pleasure," because the truth is much graver than that. You have sinned against yourself, your very essence, against the holy soul with which you were born. And as toward an obvious sin that you would always regret, you should repent for having wronged yourself.

This is the meaning of King David's words, "My sin is always before me" (Psalm 51:5). Even if my sin is only before me, it will always be a sin for me.

6

PUTTING REMORSE INTO ACTION

Remorse over a spiritual slip is positive only if it is followed and complemented by acts of repentance. Otherwise it may even have a negative effect.

This is because by nature, human emotions are fleeting: they come and then they go. Thus, the feeling of remorse and anxiety, if not expressed in the world of action and reinforced through a real act of repentance, will just pass and cease to be. Instead of remorse you will just feel relief, relief from the pangs of remorse. You may then think that your relief is your soul's joy at having rid itself of the cause of remorse. But this is not so; your soul is still ill, full of unrealized remorse.

This is what our Sages meant by "Sinful people are full of remorse."

7

SWIMMING AGAINST PUBLIC
OPINION

As a torrent river surges forth, sweeping
with it all that lies in its path, penetrating into deep
recesses and washing away all buried things, so does the
torrent of public opinion sweep along the individual
mind. You may not know it, you may even deny it, but
you have been brainwashed by common belief. Carried
along, perhaps more, perhaps less, you now think along
these twisted paths.

So stay away from the middle of the river, don't be
concerned with what people say. But this alone will not
protect you, because you cannot completely seclude
yourself. Who can vouch that your wife or children will
not be swept along with the flow? They will then be the
open floodgates to bring the floodwaters inside your

doors. And who can abstain from breathing the air that carries the germ of public opinion? Thoughts and opinions are beyond time and space and flow from mind to mind in quantum leaps.

Nor can you remain static in this torrent river just by standing firm in your place—you must actively swim against the flow. You may not be successful in swimming upstream, but at least you will not be swept down by the flow. So it is with the spiritual life and the purity of spirit that you have attained. You cannot retain them against the flow unless you continue to struggle for spiritual growth. You must swim upstream without respite—upward, onward against the flow. There may be a limit to how far you can go, but at least you will not be drawn down with the flow.

8

WAGING THE HOLY INNER WAR

Do not try to justify yourself by saying, "What shall I do? My baser drives are very strong and they always get the best of me." This only shows that you're not really trying.

Think for a moment: did God place you in this world just to sit back and relax and enjoy yourself? No, He placed you here to be His faithful servant and wage the battle of life on earth.

Yet do not pride yourself that your passions and temptations are a sign of your godliness: "Am I not fighting God's holy war against these drives that He placed in me?" Because who can vouch that your passions are God-sent and not just your own earthliness. Even in *Gehinnom* you will only be compelled to continue living the life that you yourself chose while on earth. Who knows? Perhaps your entire earthly life is some form of hell.

This is how you can judge yourself. If whenever your passions rise to attack you, you smite them back a double blow, not only do you ignore their demands but you perform instead a *mitzvah* as well.[1] Then you can know that you are among God's elite forces who have been chosen to fight His war—be happy to have your inner enemy as well.

But if you humbly surrender to the onslaught of your passions without declaring an all-out war, then you should mourn not only for your falling in battle but also for merely having your passions. Your entire life is just an eternal hell where you are compelled to do as you choose.

---

[1] See Rashi on *Sanhedrin* 111b, *U'mitgaber*.

9

THE NEED FOR STIMULATION

The human soul relishes sensation, not only if it is a pleasant feeling but for the very experience of stimulation. Sooner sadness or some deep pain rather than the boredom of nonstimulation. People will watch distressing scenes and listen to heartrending stories just to get stimulation. Such is human nature and a need of the soul, just like all its other needs and natures. So he who is clever will fulfill this need with passionate prayer and Torah learning.

But the soul whose divine service is without emotion will have to find its stimulation elsewhere. It will either be driven to cheap, even forbidden sensation or will become emotionally ill from lack of stimulation.

10

BECOMING WHO YOU REALLY ARE

People are always bemoaning what seems to them to be their lack of freedom of choice. They feel so compelled by earthly desires that they feel they cannot control themselves. But know that for every choice that must emerge from an individual chooser himself, there must be an individuated self to choose. There must be a person who can stand by himself, who can decide what he wants for himself. But if there is no person, just one of the crowd, there can be no free choice or personal will. Because who will choose if, besides the herd mentality, there is no one there at all?

So look deep inside to see if you have individuated your real self. Are you a person who can stand by himself or are you just a member of the human species?

Are you like a plant or an animal whose individual essence is just one of the kind? What is in the species is in the specimen, which is why they have no free will. Their instincts are not under their individual control but under that of the collective laws of the species. Their willfulness does not rise out of individual need but out of collective need of the species.

The Essence of Individuation

But how is a person individuated from mankind— by differentials in intelligence or willfulness? No, this cannot be—animals also have differentials of this kind. At its prime, an animal has greater strength, willfulness, and perhaps even intelligence than when aged. Nevertheless, the basic nature encompasses them all, without the ability of individual choice.

So a person must individuate himself with the essence of who he really is: not only must he not remain imprisoned by social rules, cultural customs, or accepted thought without the ability to see beyond them but he must also have a mind of his own. Without this, not only is he not a Jew but he is also not even a person.

This means bringing out that which is unique within you, that which depicts your very self. Your Torah learning or divine service should be not just an expression of your intelligence but of your very essence as well. The way you approach Torah learning or prayer should represent you. When someone hears a Torah thought or a specific spiritual practice, let him be able to identify it as typically one of yours.

Take for instance the Rambam's works—they can be identified by their style and distinct wisdom. The same is true of the Ramban's. This is so because each of them expressed his unique and essential self through the vehicle of Torah wisdom.

Individuation Is Your Obligation

And this is not some privilege reserved only for the great luminaries. Rather, each and every little one of us has not only the right but the obligation to express his unique and individual self. And to the degree that you are able to live in this world from the very center of your unique self, to that degree will you be able to exercise your individual free will.

Raise yourself up above the crowd; bring out what makes you unique. Become a person who can choose for himself—the prerequisite for reaching God.

11

THE DYNAMICS OF PASSIONATE EMOTIONS

When a person has not prepared himself for the spiritual afterlife, when he departs he will be exposed to the naked experience of a wasted life. These are called the "naked souls" who, spiritually homeless, must enter the spiritual netherworlds.

But even in this life, when a person sins and channels his passions in the wrong direction, parts of his soul already enter into the spiritual netherworlds. And even if he doesn't sin, just does not channel his passions into spiritual service, with no outlet of holiness in which to go, his passions will fall toward the netherworlds. These parts of his soul, his potential passion for God, are transformed into baser passions.

The greater the soul, the greater the danger if he

does not channel his passions Godward. His greater soul with its greater passions remains naked, and his passions will go somewhere else.

So as sitting back and refraining from sin is tantamount to doing a *mitzvah* (*Kiddushin* 39b), sitting back and not serving God with passion is sometimes tantamount to a transgression.

12

LEAVING YOUR MARK ON THE WORLD

He who knows his place.

Be creative and contribute to the world, give it the best you have. Make a niche for yourself that will always be felt in the world.

Are not the "places" of our forefathers, the prophets, and other *tzaddikim* to this day not known in the world? What a void there would be in the world if, for instance, there had been no Baal Shem Tov?

So "he who knows his place"—who leaves a mark in this world with his life—his "place" will forever be known, even beyond his life.

13

THE ULTIMATE PROOF OF GOD

ertainly you have heard of or seen the books that deal with the existence of God. For those who find it hard to believe, they try to prove that there is a God. They bring their proofs from Creation itself, its inherent wisdom and almighty nature. But woe for you if you need their proofs.

Have you not felt, have you not seen, how your soul is so sure it sees God? You speak to Him in second person both in formal and informal prayer because the truth is that your soul does see Him present, right there before you.

And when your soul cries out in pain, "I shall not fear because You are with me" (Psalm 23:4), you feel as if you are clinging to God, Who then will heal your soul. Or when you yearn or pour out your soul, you say, "God! Please bring me closer! Help me to surrender my very self to You, because I yearn greatly to come closer."

So why do you need abstract proof that God exists if your soul knows and sees for itself? King Shlomo said that abstract wisdom is for fools and the empty-hearted (Proverbs 1:20, 9:4), because who needs proof beyond personal experience—only the fools and the empty-hearted.

14

IS IT WISH OR IS IT RESOLUTION?

If you want to know if you've progressed on your spiritual path over the years, the way to judge is to look at your resolution—at your inner drive—and not at your wishes.

Only the inner drive with which you work to attain your desired goal is called resolution. But if you do not work but rather just want, this is not called resolution. It is just some wish that you wish for yourself to be blessed with that desired objective. For example, the pauper who works to sustain himself, this is a drive, because he is doing something constructive toward it. But the wish that he'll find a million dollars is just a wish to be rich and not a resolution.

Every Jew would like to be a *tzaddik*, but this is no

more than a wish: he'd like to wake up in the morning and suddenly find himself a *tzaddik*. Only the level and state of being that you seriously work toward can truly be called a resolution.

Therefore a wish can be for great things and be way out of line with reality: to find some great treasure, to be transformed to some great saint, to spontaneously change reality.

But the true inner drive that is accompanied with hard work is not for jumping but for gradual progress. Step after step to a higher level is the goal of those driven from within. Consequently, the objective of your resolution will be in direct proportion to your present spiritual level: at the beginning your strivings will be to master lower levels, and as you progress, your drive will be to attain progressively higher levels.

So if you want to know how you've progressed and to gauge the change in your spiritual level, compare the goal of your drive of last year with that for which you strive now: is it for the same objectives or even for higher? This shall be your sign that, thank God, you have made progress.

15

PERSONAL RULES FOR SPIRITUAL GROWTH—I

I f you have been able to draw up personal rules for your spiritual growth, consider this a success. But if you have not, then either you have not devoted your life to personal growth or you are blind to your own failures and successes.

Because the spiritual seeker who channels his efforts to his inner world will inevitably be faced with difficulty and distraction—not only external ones like supporting his family but also in his inner world such as indolence, negative tendencies, destructive character traits, and so forth—and because the spiritual seeker is constantly involved in this inner battle, sometimes winning and sometimes losing, he will inevitably come to conclusions: which strategies work for him and which ones bring out his weakness.

So someone who cannot draw such conclusions is not engaged in the battle—he neither wins nor loses. Or else he is unaware of both his inner weaknesses and strong points.

16

LOATHING YOUR NEGATIVE NATURE—I

You cannot ward off your negative drives unless you also hate them. An intent to just not welcome them is not enough—you must actively despise them. They can destroy your life, both spiritual and physical.

So train yourself to become enraged when negative drives cloud your mind or emotions. Only then will you be able to control them. When our Sages said, "Develop a wrath toward your baser nature" (*Berakhot* 5a), they meant it literally—wrath and vexation.

17

FACING GOD AFTER CONFRONTING DEATH

A terror came over me yesterday during *Shalosh Seudos* as the thought came to mind: what would happen if my demise were nearby? The *Mishnah* says to repent one day before one's death (*Avot* 2:15). I wonder how I could do it. Just to refrain from forbidden behavior and thought by simply controlling oneself is possible even at the prime of one's life—just keep in mind your possible imminent demise. But to really change everything that needs change and to heal all wounds of my soul the way I know I really should and indeed want to—this is not so easy to do.

So when I think about what would be if I were suddenly called before God with all these blemishes on my soul, I become gripped by panic and terror—I am not nearly as afraid of death, even a premature one, as I am afraid of this specter.

But the truth is, why am I afraid to face God just in higher worlds with my blemished soul and not embarrassed to face Him on earth? Who knows? Perhaps God has already rejected my soul and banished it far out of His Presence.

There is nothing left for me to do other than to cry out to Him: "God! Save me because I'm drowning!"

18

A JOURNEY INTO CREATION

Have you ever experienced the bliss of prayer pure of ulterior motive or personal interests? Have you ever cried before God as you uttered His praises or been greatly aroused when speaking to Him? Did you feel then His Presence pressing through the limits of your heart and mind, and you yourself could not grasp or understand it? Any tears you will shed during your prayers are like those of a child crying for a toy or a sweet as long as these experiences are beyond you.

This, then, is the way to reach them if you want to: let go of this world for an hour or two—its hustle and bustle, its cunning deceptions, and all your earthly aspirations. Seclude yourself in privacy—go out into a forest if possible. Let yourself become a simple creature in God's world. With the sun, the moon, the birds, and the trees, sing songs of praise to Him. Reveal the greatness of God to the world, and fill it with a sense of that greatness.

In this state of mind, begin by reciting: "*Adon Olam*—Master of the Universe . . ." "*Yedid Nefesh*—Beloved Companion of my being. . . ." See how your soul then rushes out to greet the approach of its Maker. God has come, so to speak, to hear your sweet song, and a holy passion engulfs you. Only the gushing of your warm tears will be able to calm your passion.

Then you will know why Moshe prayed to become a bird of the sky after his passing (*Genesis Rabbah* 11:9): he yearned to sing praise to God as a simple creature before Him.

19

THE REBBE'S MIDLIFE TRANSITION

hank God, I am already in my fortieth year of life and in a few months it will be my fortieth birthday. After that begins the decline of life, the beginnings of my old age. I am afraid. Very afraid. Not so much from the inevitable passing of my life but from the spiritual poverty of my years do I shudder: they are gone and past, empty and void, wasted on childish games.

"What will be with you, mortal creature!" I tell myself. "Your prime of life is gone, and now, when you've reached your decline, when the inevitable process of dying has begun, only now you remember your Creator?"

And even now, can I be sure of myself? How many

periods of inspiration and improvement have I already had in my life, and what always happened to them? They passed like snow on a summer's day. This happened at previous transitions of life: before my *bar mitzvah*, before my wedding. . . . I experienced then such a deep inspiration and felt so firm in my convictions. I said to myself that from then on I was certain to be God's faithful servant. And who knows if even now, once I become accustomed to being past forty, that the past will not happen again: all the inspiration and aspiration will melt and disappear. As there is no trace left from my earlier inspirations, what will be left of this one?

But I dare not despair! My heart pounds from my impending fortieth birthday, my entire body shakes from my oncoming declining years. Still, I will try to muster all my strength to commit myself and my life to God. Perhaps, perhaps something will remain.

Just One Thing Missing

But to what shall I commit myself? To learn more? I think that as far as possible, I don't waste any time. To abstain from physical pleasures? If my own desires are not fooling me, thank God, I am not so attached to them. So what am I missing? Simply to be a Jew. I see myself as a self-portrait that shows all colors and features real to life. Just one thing is missing: the soul.

"God! Master of the World, Who sees my innermost secrets! Before You I confess. You I beseech! I feel so cast aside and distanced from You and from Your holy Presence! Help me—I want to become a simple Jew!

"God! Save me from wasting the rest of my years chasing the illusions of life! Draw me closer and bring me into Your innermost Presence! Bind me to You forever and ever in wealth of spirit and soul!"

20

BECOMING THE MASTER OF YOUR OWN LIFE

wo weeks ago, I nearly decided not to pray anymore for long life. I had been perturbed by the old age of a certain old Jew that can be more aptly called a condemnation.

His entire life he had been a *chasid*, meticulous like all his chasidic peers. Then, when he reached sixty, his baser drives grabbed him by the neck and compelled him to act them out in the latrine. And he sank there, deeper and deeper, for many, many years. Even when he was seventy-five years old, he could not control himself and refrain from his shameful behavior. Yet how he can still delude himself that he is a respectable old *chasid* is an enigma to me.

Is old age like this, submerged in spiritual filth, to

be called a life we should look forward to reach? Or is this spiritual putrefaction in the depths of Hell from which we should flee as far as we can?

The Fighting Spirit

An awesome terror grips me as I think about this. God! Just living and getting old is such a hazard!

We have spoken about this elsewhere, but I will recapitulate the point: the state of any individual's purity and character is dependent on his fighting spirit. Two people can be plagued by equally base drives, yet one will overcome them and the other be overcome by them. He who can muster his inner strength and say, "I am the master of my life," will be able to overcome his drives. Another whose heart is weak and whose spirits are wilted will be overwhelmed by the slightest impulse.

"Who is the true strong man?—he who can control his desires" (*Avot* 4:1). Only the strong of spirit are able to control their desires. Therefore, when a person ages and his strength of spirit wanes, he will find it harder to control himself. His only saving grace is that his baser drives also wane with his body strength. But woe to the unfortunate soul whose drives do not wane with his body strength: if he did not defuse them when he was young, he is in greater danger of caving in to them when he is old.

So as it is insufficient merely to act like a *chasid*, but one must *become* a *chasid*, as it is insufficient just to act with holiness, but one must *become* holy, as the verse actually says, "Act with holiness and become holy" (Leviticus 11:44, 20:7), so too is it insufficient to just act with strength of spirit. You must become strong-spirited and take possession of your inner world.

Train yourself to be the master of all aspects of your life, not only regarding forbidden behavior, not only regarding permissible pleasure, but regarding your entire inner life. Let not any natural response be triggered in spontaneous fashion, be it action, a refrain from action, speech, or even thought. Become the absolute and ultimate master of your inner world so that it reacts not to external influence but only to your deepest command.

If you train yourself in your younger years, you will become a giant of spirit. Your body may age, your physical strength may wane, but your inner essence, your spirit, will remain strong. To the end of your life you will be able to take pride in your continuing spiritual victories.

21

A "JEWISH HEART" IS NOT ENOUGH

Many people console themselves by saying, "Well, if I am not serving God as I should and am not as refined as behooves me, at least I have good aspirations. Many times my heart cries out in the pain of my distance from Him."

But would the drowning person console himself with his desire to rescue his life and with his heart's cry facing imminent death? What use is it if he doesn't act to save himself and try to get out of the water?

22

CLEARING YOUR MIND OF DISTRACTION

In order to be able to raise your spiritual level, you must first be able to let go of your worries. Throw away all your troubling luggage, at least for the time you devote to spiritual growth. Even if you then experience a sudden leap only to fall right back down to your normal level, it will be easier thereafter to return at times to that higher state and maybe even to eventually remain there.

But someone who is so attached to his earthly life that he can never put aside his preoccupations is unlikely to be able to raise himself to higher spiritual states of being, whether by gradual progress or in quantum leaps.

23

PUTTING YEARNING INTO ACTION

earning is of value only if you put it into action as a driving force for reaching higher levels. Otherwise, it will tend to create within you a subtle despair. Without your being aware of it, you will be feeling, "I have been yearning for so many years and have accomplished nothing. I must have no further potential." In the end, you will stop yearning.

24

ENVISIONING YOUR IDEAL SPIRITUAL SELF

If you have already tried everything without success, if you have tried to rouse your soul with all your means but it has not been aroused to lead the conscious life that it should and to yearn for the spiritual life that behooves it, this is what you should do:

Envision yourself as already the ideal spiritual person you really are. Just imagine the greatness of your soul . . . see how your soul shines in God's garden, in Eden, as He comes to enjoy your company with His holy entourage. . . .

Meditate deeply on these pictures. . . . Hold these images in your mind's eye. . . . Inevitably you will be roused to a higher awareness. . . . You do not want to sully your soul. . . . Savor the bliss of embrace by the great Creator as you yearn to actualize this from the depths of your soul.

25

WHEN MEANING IN LIFE IS LOST

Don't mourn only for those who kill themselves; mourn even more for those who kill their lives.

People are bemoaning the cheapness of life and those who have committed suicide.[1] I, though, worry even more for the living. He has not killed himself, nevertheless he is dead. Life has become so meaningless to him that living and dying are the same.

Until now, for a Jew to flaunt God's laws, he'd first have to renounce his faith in ultimate judgment. But now I see believing Jews who still are living wanton

---

[1]From 1926 to 1928 many Jews were losing their livelihoods and the number of suicides was rising.

lives. This is only because their self-esteem is so eroded and destroyed that life, death, Heaven, and Hell have all become meaningless. Who is it all for, anyway—for a self that seems too worthless and insignificant to make any effort?

Apathy. Apathy for everything, even for one's very being.

26

SHALOSH SEUDOS:
THE WEEKLY YOM KIPPUR—I

It amazes me why people don't get as excited about going to the weekly *Shalosh Seudos* as they do about going to *Kol Nidre*.

It has sometimes happened to me at a *Shalosh Seudos* that I don't know where I've been until now: I feel as if I have been hidden away somewhere or that I have hidden myself from facing God, and suddenly here I am—standing before Him face-to-face. I feel that God is then looking straight at me, His awareness penetrating right through me. His penetrating vision seems to spot and bear witness to my every blemish.

I am gripped by shame and terror. I would try to hide myself among the crowd of people, maybe under the table, but where can I hide from God? Wherever I hide, there You are. My secret refuge is filled with Your Presence. And when I reach the singing of the Twenty-third Psalm—"I shall not fear for You are with me"— my tongue freezes and is unable to continue. How dare I leave my shelter of shame to identify with God and say "for You are with me"? I feel at that moment that God is looking upon me with such censuring pity that it eats up my heart and stings my entire body.

And sometimes I am overwhelmed by such a shame that I almost lose all my spirits. I then clearly see my lowly state of being—whatever good points I may have are nothing when experiencing God's Presence. I then feel like a lowly worm that brags about how strong and beautiful its holes in the ground are until it sees the palaces built by humans. What a joke all its under-ground tunnels are compared to the palaces of humans! Whatever holiness and purity of soul I am capable of attaining are nothing before the Ultimate Pure Being. How insignificant they are before Him to Whom even the heavens are unrefined.

Yet none of these feelings were new insights—I had known it all before. But then, I only knew. Now, at this *Shalosh Seudos*, it was real: there was God's holy Presence right before me, pressing my very being. And in front of His dazzling Presence the peak of my enlight-enment became darkened.

My being melts away. I have lost sense of selfness; I have no existence of my own. But my soul takes courage, come what may. I cry out: "Even in the depths of Hell I shall not fear, for You are with me!"

Like the retarded son of the king who calls to his father while playing with his kind—will not the king come to fetch him? He may not be worthy of royal treatment, but rather than risk royal shame, the king will respond to his cry. That's how I feel. Whether You save me or not, my heart yearns to be close to You. To call You by name is so pleasant to me, my entire being cries out to You. My soul may be darkened, filled with impurity; still You, Father, will rush to my comfort. How can You stand by as Your Divine Name is shamed when from Hell resounds my cry, "FATHER!"

"Even in the depths of Hell I shall I not fear, for You are right there with me!"

Each *Shalosh Seudos* is different. Sometimes I only feel brokenhearted, sometimes also the ensuing self-encouragement. But when I get to singing *"Eyn K'Elokeynu"*—"There is none like our God"—my soul always becomes strengthened and contented, not out of any feeling of self-fulfillment, just out of the privilege to serve the Infinite Creator. He has appointed me, out of no merit of my own, to declare His Greatness and Oneness to Creation. My brokenheartedness is thus transformed into bliss and resolution as I declare it before all of Creation. To the heavens, the earth, to humans and lower life, even to the dust that is under my feet, I say, "Listen and I shall tell you: *Eyn K'Elokeynu!*"

And then at the peak of my bliss and resolution, the flames of my soul soar up before God: *"Atah Hu Elokeynu*—You are our Master!"

Finally, when the *Shabbat* has passed its climax and candles are brought to light up the night, I find myself a different person. I realize how necessary it all was: the brokenheartedness at the beginning and the bliss that came afterward are one process, one purification.

So I continue to wonder why people don't get as excited about going to the weekly *Shalosh Seudos* as they do about going to *Kol Nidre*.

27

THE REBBE'S SOMERSAULTS

When a Jewish person reveals from within himself his inherent holiness with which to serve his Creator, then every act that he does for God, even self-initiated service, becomes for that while actually holy. And these physical acts, done in divine service, will in turn sanctify his physical body.

How else can you explain why I became so enthused when I decided to somersault in honor of the *Sefer Torah*? Why else did my whole body become so energized when I saw the place where I would dance and my whole body shook with excitement?

Frequently a Jew's yearning is ignited far beyond the normal level of his service. His soul then yearns to perform some great act for God, but his heart is broken from the reality of his normal service. And even when his soul is not inflamed to actual self-sacrifice, it yearns for self-transcendence: if only now I were able to perform some act that would lift me out of myself. If only now I were able to extract my very being from my normal self, I would soar up straight to the heavens.

When I started preparing myself to attend the *Sefer Torah* dedication ceremony, my yearning already had begun to flare. The thought that such an awesomely holy and joyous occasion might come only once in my lifetime started to burn within me. I wanted very much to do something for God. "Right! I will rejoice in awe and dance with all my might. No, that may be nice, but my soul is still not pacified. This is not the great act suitable for such an awesome occasion."

Rebutting Self-doubt

Then the idea came to me to somersault as the lowly peasants do for their masters. But a countervoice spoke up within me: "What kind of service are you trying to do; what is the reason for it? Do you really think it matters to God whether or not you do somersaults? And perhaps you might even hurt yourself or damage your health. Will you not look like a fool doing somersaults in front of all those people?"

Then from the depths of my heart I screamed at this voice: "God destroy you, forces of evil! This is no time for second thoughts—the moment is great, it is unique, and it is passing. To do some act of self-sacrifice for God is what I want, and you have only helped me to find it. The very act that you seek to intimidate me from doing because of health or personal reasons, that is the act I choose to do and I now hallow myself in preparation."

From that moment on, this self-contrived, unsophisticated act became for me a holy service. It was now very clear in my eyes and I surrendered myself completely to it. My conscious thoughts had just begun to wonder how I would somersault, when the flames of my soul engulfed me to self-sacrifice. No more did I imagine any simple somersault, but now God's altar shone before me. The place where the procession was about to pass became hallowed with the flames of holy fire. I felt as if my blood were bubbling while my tears were pouring forth.

By whom and how did this simple act become hallowed for the moment? Why did my entire body shake with fervor and become then also hallowed? It must be my "sparks," my potential spiritual energy, that were now being expressed in reality. The simplest Jew has such sparks. I greatly rejoiced later on to learn that King David also somersaulted before the Holy Ark (*Numbers Rabbah* 4:20, *Etz Yosef*).

Rebutting Postmortems

But maybe I did fool myself. Maybe my act did not become hallowed for the moment. Maybe it was all my own imagination. The truth is that I did not have the spiritual experience I anticipated and the state of being I felt so sure to attain, I did not. But God help me from such self-doubt—this is also a self-destructive maneuver, to question what one feels and sees. How can one deny a real inner experience? I know that every time I sit down to learn, I feel God's Presence around me. It feels as if His Light is filling my mind, my heart, my very innards and even deeper. Was it not being moved by this feeling that I decided to sing *Adon Olam*? I was sure my ego would dissolve, my very being would melt, and I would become filled instead with God's Presence. The entire world would then be for me just a spark of God, shining from His brilliance.

Yes, I did not attain what I felt sure I would. I guess I do not yet know myself. I may feel that I am aware of my lowly level, but I must be still ego-driven: I expected more than my capability. Nevertheless, what I did experience was real, because even the self-contrived service of the simplest Jew becomes hallowed for the moment.

28

LEVELS OF SPIRITUAL EXPERIENCE

Would you like to measure your spiritual experience, your awe of God and depth of your inner vision? Would you like to know if you really found your innermost soul and with it peeked at God through the cosmic spectrum? Did you see Him Who cannot be seen and grasp Him Who is beyond physical dimensions? Did you see Him Who is exalted beyond all worlds and gaze at His blinding hidden Light? Did you really experience these things, or was it all in your mind and imagination?

This, then, shall be your test: did you feel, while meditating, detached from your normal self, uplifted to a higher perspective . . . so intense was your surrender and selflessness then that you feared even to fear or love God? . . . Did you melt from the sweat that drenched

your body and feel ashamed to even pray to Him, the
supreme and transcendent Being? . . . Did you see Him
Who is indwelling, though you know you didn't? Did
you recognize Him as the Unrecognizable? . . . Did you
pray only with great effort and out of a broken heart,
shame, and humility, and did so just to fulfill His
will? . . . If this transpired, then you transcended your
self—you saw through the eyes of your soul. If you did
not experience any of these things, then you saw only
with your mind's eye. But do not stop meditating even
if this is your limit, because this, too, is very worth-
while.

70

29

THE COSMIC SECRET

Your mysteries, great universe, I do not know, nor do I even dare to ponder. If I just set apart one aspect of your mysterious oneness, thinking that I could understand it, what a fool indeed I would be! But when I perceive your entirety as a secret of God, with each of your phenomena a phenomenal secret, when I see myself as a fool who is trying to be wise, then I can glimpse your secret. Your mystery, great universe, is the mystery of God, and when I see that, I am from the few initiates.

The holy Baal Shem Tov used to say that to behold you is to behold God, your Master. As for me, though, I have never beheld such visions and your Master I have never seen. But this much I have peeked at and I can vouch for: God is hidden in your secret. Not only the hiddenness, God's apparent absence, did I see but I have seen both the concealment and the revelation: I saw that the dark secret itself is the revealment. Only when I saw you as a secret could my soul grasp you and be enlightened. But if I relied on my mind to analyze and understand you, then my experience would disappear. No more visions, no more illumination. Just darkness, cosmic darkness.

Why do you, universe, so hide yourself to let so many be fooled by your material surface? Why don't you just reveal yourself as the window to the palace of God? Why do you make it such an effort for us and such torment for the searching soul? Remove your curtain and let me enter into the chambers of God's palace.

With awesome quiet and cosmic silence, your unceasing message resounds without noise. To behold you is like beholding a great *tzaddik* deep in meditation. Your eternal hush grips us with awe as your total surrender to God's existence draws us also into that rapture.

Blissful is the person who serves God with your substance, fusing physical action with right intention. Merging the material with the spiritual, he serves the one God together with you.

Worlds . . . beyond worlds . . . beyond worlds all together . . . levels . . . below levels . . . below levels all declare: "From the cosmos to beyond . . . to above . . . and below . . . there is nothing except for God."

30

THE POWER OF JEWISH JOY
AND TEARS

A record of some thoughts and feelings from the High Holidays and Festivals of 1933, especially from the dancing.

"God! Do You not hear our cries? What will You do with the countless Jewish tears that were shed during these past Days of Awe? What will You do with the oceans of Jewish tears spilled over the last two decades? During the past twenty-five hundred years? Have these waters of holy passion been, God forbid, lost like rivers into the ocean? And what are You doing with all Your own tears, so to speak, that You shed every day over our desolation and our affliction?

"God! Intimate and Immanent Creator! You have created worlds beyond worlds, and in each You have created countless creatures. Yet in all the vast infinite-ness of Your universes, only man have You created to serve You. All of the others do not really serve You and cannot proclaim You as the ultimate Master.

"And out of all mankind, it is only the Jew who, with his heart and soul, is ready to serve You. Merciful Father, we bear suffering to serve You, and You seem to watch from the distance! Our souls pour forth with our tears in order to serve You, and You seem to watch with impassion! The entire world derides us and beats us because we refuse to deny You—are You, too, going to beat us? We seek asylum from holocausts in Your Presence—are You to then conceal Your holy Presence? We lift our spirits by calling to our Father in Heaven—are You then to shut out our cries by closing the gates of Heaven?

"Surely we have sinned and You have many claims against us, but God!—let our prosecutors bear witness: throughout all the cosmos only Your Jewish People rose to say *Selichot*! Who but Your Jewish People resounded the *shofar* throughout the heavens, and who so enlightened the upper worlds with Yom Kippur, *sukkah*, and *lulav* if not Your Jewish People?

The Infinite One within Me

"Heavenly prosecutors! How dare you lay claim against the Jewish People? Are you not awed to stand in front of the lowliest of our People? It is not before him that you should tremble but before the infinite One Who resides in him. Throughout this endless, dark, and bitter exile, when it seemed that Jewish service was indeed undesired in Heaven; when it seemed that even our best souls were unworthy of consideration; when the entire world stands up together to destroy me, as if from His Presence God Himself has cast me; when darkness has covered the face of the earth with no prophet to brighten our sullen hearts and no seer to lift our broken spirits; when only fear can fill the heart of the onlooker and terror grips the mind of the thinker—then if any Jew retains faith in God and continues to do his best in His service, this cannot be any human spirit but the power of the infinite One in me! Heavenly prosecutors, bear witness to this: our devotion surpasses that of all heavenly creatures! The infinite God, the unlimited One, resides even in our children and this explains it. Honor the One Who resides within us and dare you not lay claim against the Jewish People!

"And all you departed souls—forefathers! prophets! saintly people!—how can you keep silent at this time? Who enlightened the heavenly *Gan Eden* if not us on earth with our recent service? Whence came your dancing on this recent Simchat Torah more than on any other day—are you not now in worlds beyond time? It must be that the dancing of the earthly Jew has aroused you also to dancing." Because when the Jewish people rejoice, the essence of the Jewish soul is aroused. This collective Jewish soul, this great cosmic soul, whose source is the forefathers and encompasses the simplest Jew, then rejoices and dances around God.

And can it be otherwise? Can our great, lowly service of joy on earth not give joy to God and our dancing before Him not arouse all souls and spiritual beings to dance with us?

Throughout the year, the Jew carries the heavy burden of divine service. How much effort it is then to rejoice on earth with God on Simchat Torah! Perhaps only after the uplifting Days of Awe that precede it is the Jew able to perform such a feat.

Joy starts to enter, but the heart still cries, "How can a Jew now rejoice?! The Jewish People and, so to speak, You Yourself, are so sunken in sorrow and affliction!" But then comes a voice of encouragement: "With my God I am now rejoicing! The exalted Creator Who is beyond all worlds, Whom the highest angels cannot fathom, He is the intimate God of my soul, of my spirit, and of my flesh. It is with Him and His Torah, which He gave me with love, that I will now dance and rejoice."

Nothing now exists: no world, no worries, no earthly life with its sorrows. With all my might I will now dance, and with God Himself will I rejoice before Him.

God! You Bear Witness

But still deep inside, discontent murmurs, "And what do you think makes you a Jew? What kind of a relationship do you have with God that you now dance and rejoice before Him? Was your divine service befitting the name of service of the Infinite? And what of your soul, your Jewish soul? Did you treat it as befits a divine spark? How then do you have the audacity to rejoice with the infinite God?"

This voice you must answer strongly: "Do you want to estrange me from my God? Are you trying to destroy my relationship with Him?

"God! You bear witness: I am always prepared to sacrifice myself for You! True, my service compared to Your greatness is not even worthy of Your consideration, but I stand ready to sacrifice my life to You, God, and for Your glory. For this, God, I am able to muster all my might and to dance and rejoice before You: 'Blissful be the Jew! Blissful be the Jew! Blissful be the Jew!' "

The soul becomes filled with what it cannot grasp and rejoices though it knows not why. The mind is now empty of all comprehension—images and sensations are all gone. The existence of God and inexplicable bliss are all that now fill Creation. . . . "We are the chosen who received His Torah . . . in the desert . . . an undeserved present." And this is the bliss, the intimate union we experience when all barriers between God and Creation disappear in the bliss of the moment.

Jewish Blood and Tears

"And you, heavenly beings, angels of God, who see spiritual concepts as we see the material—have you ever seen a being as sublime as the Jew? For you our thoughts are tantamount to action, so tell us what you see on this day: a Jew stands in *shul* on Simchat Torah sacrificing his very life while at the same time singing and dancing!

"Not just the sweat that falls from his brow and the joyous tears can you see and bear witness to. But blood you see, Jewish blood flowing, as he dances and sings while in slaughter!

"Now let me ask you, if you rejoice with us, why are you silent to our sorrows? How long do you keep quiet and restrain yourselves? We have no more strength to continue! Forefathers, saints, from all generations! Rise up on our behalf! Collect our tears shed in joy and remorse, and bring them straight to God! Incite all the worlds until God sees and returns us to intimacy! Let all the worlds know our plight until God fills the needs of our flesh and our souls!"

And why are the rivers and oceans of holy passion themselves lying silent? Who brought their roar to a whisper? Because when their fomentation begins, the rivers roar, the oceans' waves rage, and they all declare: "Come, let us uproot all Jewish enemies! Bring us to whoever dares to harm the lowliest Jew and we will wash him away like the soil!"

And beyond the roar of the waves, the storm, and

the thunder, God Himself cries in anguish. While in Heaven, the ministers of the gentile nations then fear that the Day of Reckoning has come; on earth, the nations are at war. In darkness they lived and in darkness they will die, cast down to the bottom of Hell. And as Jewish tears are purging and flooding the world, a still voice is heard in Jewish hearts: "Soon, soon will come the *Mashiach*!"

Who then can calm these stormy waters and prevent them from fulfilling their mission? Why after the Great War has the world gone back to its frivolous folly, while we Jews have returned to our sorrows? They all make merry while we sit in shame. They all make money while we sit abjectly and wallow.

"Please, God! Hear the voice of our cries! Have pity on Yourself, so to speak, and on us—Your children and servants. Draw us out of the darkness and near to You! True, what are our actions, our repentance and penance before You Whose holy angels tremble with awe? Who is really worthy of Your Presence? But still, have we not purified our very souls by immersing in the oceans of our tears? See how each one of us, when outpouring his bitter soul, is at the same time rejoicing in Your Presence, totally surrendering his very essence to Your will and cleaning his mind of any unwanted presence. No slightest thought will now enter my mind to spoil the bliss of this moment. All is now Light and holiness. . . . My very being I surrender to this Light. Is our immersing in these holy waters not enough even for our low level in order that we enter Your Presence?

"God! We rely on Your justness and rejoice in Your salvation!"

31

WITH EVERY THREAD
OF MY BEING

od! I praise You with my life, I extol You with my being" (Psalm 146:2).

"Intimate Creator! I yearn greatly to experience Your holiness. I long to praise Your great Name. And even beyond the extent of my longing, I offer to You my very being to continuously sanctify Your Name.

"Because what is the extent of my desire to praise You? Is it at least equal to that of my self-preservation? Is my desire to extol You equal to the desire of angels to offer You song? Their very beings dissolve in the bliss and awe of their holy passion, but I know how limited is my desire. I am broken by its insignificance. So if even with my service of yearning to serve You I fall so short of fullfilling my duty, how dare I approach You, infinite and ineffable Being, to as much as offer You even a grain of sand?

"So my unworthy soul takes courage, my broken spirits take heart. Together they offer to dedicate themselves to praise God even beyond the extent of my yearning. 'I shall praise You with my very life, I shall extol You even beyond the extent of my being': as long as a trace of life remains within me, even if only a thread of my being survives, I shall strive to praise You with my body, spirit, soul, and the soul of my soul, and immerse myself in glorifying Your Name. My very essence and the source of my essence I hereby dedicate to sing Your praise.

"Because who is the person who can deceive himself into praising You just with lip service? Even were he to devote his entire life to it, how lacking it would be if it were only with his physical mouth. He must bring his soul into divine service and also come in touch with the soul of his soul. 'I shall praise God with my life, I shall extol Him with my being'—with my entire existence.

"How then, my soul, do you deceive me with being close to God? If it were so, would not my body become inflamed with holy passion for Him? Is it that my soul and the soul of my soul have been soiled by my physical body? Because if a mound of earth, Mount Sinai, blazed with Heaven's fire, why does my higher-than-that-of-angels Jewish soul not transform my physical body into spirit?

"I am filled with fear. Why are there times that I must actively rouse myself to God? I am shaking with fright. God! I am afraid even to think about the state and source of my soul. How can it be that my physical limbs do not melt at the song of the source of my soul and always burn with holy passion?

"God! Please rouse my soul! Source of my soul in

the heavens, rouse to God, the Most Exalted. Sanctify Him Who is so immanent and yet so transcendent. My spirit and my lower soul flare up and seethe with excitement. Dedicate yourselves to sanctify God forever and for all eternity. And as long as a trace of my body remains, may it not silence from declaring God's Greatness. All together may they sing: '*Kadosh, Kadosh, Kadosh*, is God of the hosts. . . .'

Seeing God in Creation

"Please, God! I am not trying now to relate the infinite wonders of Your great works, because who is the finite human who can define the infinite Being? And for man to do the superhuman, even for the infinite Creator would be a great wonder. Neither dare I try to define You with definitions of Your wonders.[1]

"Can I compare myself, God, Father and Master, to Your great righteous servants of previous generations? They experienced so intimately Your infinitely simple Light, so immanent and yet so transcendent, that they perceived no dichotomy between it and Creation.[2]

---

[1]Someone who does not see that even the spiritual light is only a divine garment and instead identifies God with that garment is only abstracting the wonders of God's work into a concept and conferring it as a title on the Creator. Thus, the mightiness is abstracted from God's mighty works and God Himself is erroneously called the "Almighty."

[2]This is because God existed before Creation and He exists since Creation—for Him there is absolutely no difference. The difference is only for us. This does not mean that for God Creation is nonexistent, because He *did* create it. What it does mean can be compared to a metaphor. A child who hears a story hears only the actual story until he is enlightened to its wisdom and metaphoric lesson. Then his consciousness rises, but he still perceives two things: the simple story and its metaphoric lesson. He even will have to remind himself from time to time of the connection

"They were able to compare Creation to its Creator, and even in what they also saw as this physical world, they saw nothing but Your emanations and Your existence, as if they were in the highest of worlds.[3]

"And in their great holiness, what were simple rocks for simple people were for them precious holy stones. They set them in Your holy coronet, and with them they adorned Your royal crown. Flaming torches of Your glorious royal garments with rays of Your brilliant light they channeled into this physical world. And in everything, from the most supernal beings to the most material mass and throughout all worlds, they saw Your shining grandeur. So they praised You with descriptions of Your glory and extolled You with the grandeur of Your supreme might.[4]

---

between the story and its lesson in order to understand it more deeply. On the contrary, the wise person who has to constrict his wisdom into the story does not perceive any difference. The story is really only the language with which he can express his wisdom. Perhaps this is what is meant by "Great is the power of the prophets who are able to compare Creation to its Creator" (*Genesis Rabbah* 27:1). Even this world they perceived as no different from the highest of divine emanations, but all as one great cosmic divine garment. And this, even though Creation was for them also Creation, nevertheless they saw it only as the metaphors for the divine light and emanations.

[3]In the highest worlds of emanation, God's existence and His life-giving emanations are intimately bound together as one. Although consciously even these great people did not grasp this transcendent level, nevertheless a definite experience of it was revealed to and through them, albeit beyond their own conscious awareness.

[4]These were not only metaphors and allusions but descriptions of the actual light. This is what the Talmud is referring to when it says, "If not that Moshe had praised God as the Great, the Almighty, and the Awesome, and that the Sages of the Great Assembly had instituted them in the standard text of prayer, we

"Their very beings expressed praise for God and manifested Your royal grandeur. They enlightened others' darkness with their divine perceptions. So though others see only the material—even materializing in their minds the lights and divine descriptions of the prophets, grasping only a slight sense of these holy concepts—still their souls and hearts tremble.[5] Our righteous prophets, when describing holy concepts or praising God, were not using cryptic metaphor or talking about abstract ideas. In their great holiness, exalted above the dichotomy of Creator and Creation, they saw only one great, royal divine garment. Nothing existed for them besides God's throne of glory, so everything that is, is a torch of holy fire with which they served God, praised Him, described Him, and extolled Him. But we, and all generations like us, can only rely on their holy intentions in order for us to praise God and extol Him.

A Mighty Call

"And I, in my spiritual poverty, am so far from their holy greatness that I cannot even see the dust of their feet. And to my great distress, in this lifetime I

---

would not be able to use them to praise God" (*Berakhot* 33b). But how were they in fact allowed to use them? This is only because of what we have said before, that they perceived these lights at their source in divine emanations, where they are intimately one with God Himself.

[5]This is because when our prophets used certain terms for description, even when describing mundane things, they were not only describing abstract concepts with metaphors but were also describing the actual supernal light as it is manifested in this world. They spoke about things in this world as they exist in the world of emanations. Therefore, even someone who perceives only the material will sense with his soul the actual supernal light that is being conveyed in the words of the prophets and will tremble.

never will. So if I cannot give name to my perception of God, then for what does my soul pine? To sing the unique song of my soul and of my soul's soul and to proclaim the unique devotions of my spirit. Not only that which I comprehend, or even just that which I can imagine, but Your greatness and grandeur, which are beyond the ability of my body and tongue to know, conceive, or sing about, I am compelled to call out and proclaim.

"My soul yearns to ascend the highest of mountains and to call out at the top of my lungs: 'There is none like our God, none like our Master, none like our divine King.' And my words will emit such holy flames, and such holy waves will surge forth to sanctify the world, that from the tufts of earth under my feet to the birds that fly in the sky, all will be transformed into manifest divineness. From the grass in the ground to the stars in the heavens, the cosmos and all that's in it, all will be aroused by my call and be stilled by the great flash it created. They all will shed their individual beingness, merging into one great unit. Together they will call out with all their might: 'God is the Ruler! God is the Ruler!' Every being will be nullified and all existence will cease to be; only that great call will remain. A mighty call, incessantly resounding with continuous roar, it will pervade all with divine holiness and even transform everything into it.

With Audacity and Trepidation

"But how dare I come to transform the outside world to godliness before having transformed my own body? How can I call out to them about God when my own body is so silent? Please God, help me. God of my fathers, I want to dedicate my whole being to sanctify You as Your servant. My soul craves that from every limb—from my sole to the soul of my soul—a single voice will be heard: 'God of Israel is the King. Surrender to His ultimate power!' And as from Mount Sinai, ever since it became holy, every day a voice can be heard in our hearts drawing us nearer to You, so too have I accepted upon myself from now on to be your servant and divine agent. This is the goal of my entire life, and I shall devote day and night to it.

"And is the burnt offering of a Jew to be discounted if its donor at the time had other thoughts? His mind may not have focused on the burnt offering to God, but was that not his intent and his actions? So I hereby offer myself to Your service. Please, God, have mercy and accept me with my broken heart. And if I should forget to focus on this intent, by day or night, awake or asleep, may this slip not disqualify my devotion and service. See that my whole life, even my mundane affairs, are only a means to offer my body and soul to Your service as a burnt offering.

"From now on, God, have mercy on us! May the motions of Jewish lips and larynx in prayer and Torah learning enlighten the world with flames of heavenly fire as the motions of angels' wings resound Your Name throughout Creation. And may this light, hidden even from us, enlighten our own and the whole world's darkness.

"So accept me, please, also, together with my physical body, to become an instrument of Your divine tongue. May all my motions—those of my lips, my feet, my tongue, my hands, my larynx, and my mind—be able to express the sweet song of my soul for You and to declare Your praise and sovereignty. 'I shall praise God with my life'—with all motions and soul-levels of my life. 'I shall extol Him with my being'—as long as a trace of my being remains.

"Please, God! I know well the inferiority of my status and the lowliness of my level. I have no standing at all in your world. I am so ashamed to approach You, my being feels so melted inside, that to ask for the slightest of my needs seems to me so audacious. I tremble before You, awesome and mighty God. If the decrepit madman dressed in tatters had some inkling of his abjection, would he dare to approach the palace of a mighty and magnificent king? I feel like a worm, so lowly and squalid, so audacious to face You, almighty and transcendent King. You are beyond the highest of worlds.

"Master of the Universe, I am so awed! My heart seems to melt inside me. I find no place for me to hide from You—I shall try in the cracks of rocks, but my hands feel compelled to rip out my own hair from fear—I find there no refuge for me. Maybe I shall hide at the ocean's bottom, but even there can I hide from You? And on the contrary, why should I even want to hide from You? You Who see all, You can see that all my desires, anxiety, fears, and yearning are to approach You, to surrender to and be hallowed by Your fire.

Forever and for All Eternity

"God, my Father! Find favor in your lowly servant's prayer, who is struggling to express himself before You. Please listen to the resolute desires of my body, soul, and soul's soul—we have decided to be Your eternal servant. Like the simple servant who runs before the king announcing the king's arrival—'Here is the king! Here he is! Prostrate yourselves before him!'—accept also me, my infinite Master, to be Your eternal servant. Support me and help me to run before You, to announce and proclaim to all: 'Hurry and come forward! God is here before you! Fear His awesome greatness! Tremble before His holiness! Surrender yourselves to Him!'

"Help me, God, and find me worthy that all acts of my body, spirit, and soul resound Your coronation as King. May all my acts be an expression of my soul's song and its inspiration. May I be able to sway myself along with others to surrender to Your sovereignty, and may I always experience the bliss of surrender. Whether when rejoicing or when weeping, whether during my lifetime or when the time comes to return my soul to You, I shall not pause even for one moment. I shall sing of Your greatness and reveal Your awesomeness to the world and to all that is in it.

"God! Bind me onto Your holy chariot to always run before You. Lengthen my days and I will fill them with songs of Your awesome greatness. 'I shall praise God with my life and extol Him with my being'—as long as some aspect of my body, spirit, or soul exists in any place in Creation, I shall serve You, eternal God, forever and for all eternity. . . .''

32

SERVING GOD JUST FOR TODAY

It is much easier to devote many years to diligent learning and even to engage in maximum self-denial than it is to devote one day of your life to serve God honestly, sincerely, and properly even according to your own understanding. But who do we think we are and what great service would we do in this one day, "even according to our own understanding," that such an undertaking seems so overwhelming?

Still, this is no cause for despair or even to be lax. On the contrary: this best service that we can do for today, this is our unique life work. And the effort we put in, together with our yearning for higher, is the aim of our life work. Let us devote these to our Creator.

33

PSYCHOTIC THINKING

Why are we so amazed by the fantasy thoughts of a psychotic, wondering how such craziness enters the human mind? Why are we not equally amazed by our own delusions, which are sometimes no less than the psychotic's?

This is because each of us has one or several emotional weak points where we still have not matured: self-indulgence . . . temper tantrums . . . ego-pride. . . . Whatever it is, each one of us, in that area, has such irrational thoughts that only a born psychotic could entertain them. But we, sophisticated savants that we are, who become enraged at the slightest affront to our intelligence, are unaware of our own fantasy thoughts and entertain psychotic thinking.

Take for example someone who is stuck in ego–pride. Everything he does or says will activate some or many thoughts of ego–pride: "How clever what I just said," or "How nice what I just did," or "How so-and-so will envy me," or "Everyone will talk about me and give me my due honor." Even if what he did or said was said or done in his own privacy, nevertheless these thoughts will still be there. And after all is said and done, his actions may have been not only not clever but even foolish. So is this the intelligent, rational being who now prides himself in foolish action? And what kind of delusive thinking is it to weave up illusory conversations of others who have nothing to discuss, because they did not see his actions? The only explanation is that as far as his ego–pride is concerned, he is psychotic—no matter how intelligent and genius he may be in all other matters. Such is the case with ego–pride, but the "rational" mind has similar delusions for self-indulgence, temper tantrums, or whatever.

Self-help for Psychosis

And what advice can we give to the human being who seeks therapy for his psychosis? The hard truth is there is no complete cure that will keep every unsound thought from rising to mind, but at least you can reduce the insanity of these thoughts and keep their appearance to a minimum. The way to do this is through heightened self-awareness.

Train yourself to watch every thought that comes to mind; pay attention to all your inner self-talk. Listen to what these inner voices are saying, especially those surrounding your emotional weak points.

At the beginning this very introspection will be

with crooked vision, deluding ourselves how clever our thoughts are. But with perseverance, by the tenth time we will clearly see how irrational our thinking is and be shocked by how our sophisticated minds ever entertained such delusions. Our deified intellect will then lose its status and become an object of laughter for us. Never again will we blindly trust our mind and rely on its rationality.

These two perspectives—objective vision and loss of credence—are necessary to reach our objective. As long as my thoughts are ideal in my eyes and my thinking is for me infallible, introspection will not help because in my heart I am saying how sound and straight are my thought patterns. I will not look with detached, objective vision. But after several times of experiencing our own psychosis, after laughing at our insane thoughts, we will be able to spot one the next time it comes and be able to correct it.

34

THE REAL TREASURE

God! Intimate Father and Friend of the
Jewish People! You are my life's treasure. Your Presence is the wealth of my being; there is nothing of value
besides You. How poor is the rich man who lives
without You, despite all his earthly riches!

"Why do you people chase empty treasures? Why
do you strive to amass fortunes of earthly value? Put
aside for a moment your treasures' illusions; forget for
the while their false security. See what you have really
collected: a mound of soul-distressing spiritual squalor.

"Why do you not pity your own lives, which are
slipping away with your delusions? How can you be so
foolish as to live in the clouds in palaces filled with

earthly pleasures or ego–honor?[1] Don't you see how you are wasting your lives with false hopes, empty joys, and pipe dreams?

"Why do you sell your souls for these treasures that will not even escort you to the grave? Don't you know that as your bodies disintegrate in earth, your heirs will rejoice in those treasures? Even during life, you have nothing but your illusions, but the death of the dreamer marks the end of illusion. Nothing, nothing to take with you—not even an illusion.

"What a shock to your souls and what agony will be that first step into the beyond! You will run to find solace in your earthly securities, to play with your pastimes of life. How horrified, though, you will now be: 'For these pieces of metal and paper money—for this I have sacrificed my life?! For the empty pleasure of pride and honor—for this I have wasted my life?! How I have ruined you—my soul! my soul!—and fooled you with empty treasures! What can I hide behind now in all of Creation?—I have nothing now with which to pre-occupy myself. For this world of true existence, of reality, of the holy, I have never prepared myself. My whole earthly being, with all its hopes, has now turned to clouds of mist. I have betrayed myself, my very own soul, and now I know not where to turn. In Hell they will send me, I feel so lost! Will I ever find myself?'

The Only Hope

"Intimate Father, light of my soul! You are my only Treasure! The closeness I feel to Your immanence in my

---

[1]We are not talking here only about financial treasures but about anything a person strives to amass that serves as his life's aim and source of pleasure, although the objective itself is nothing but an illusion.

life is the only hope there is for me. Even when I endeavor to provide for my earthly needs, these are not my treasures or my goal. Sometimes, though, I give my soul a shake—when I think I've found hidden earthly striving: some earthly treasure I am striving for besides the real treasure of Your closeness. Then my heart pounds, my innards pour out, I scream at the top of my lungs: 'This is a life? What will it lead to? An eternity of putrefaction! If only I would find favor in Your eyes and a spark of Your light ignite me, then my soul would dance forever for joy.' This is my life's hope and aspiration. What else could I ask for, what else is there to request, if my Father, my Creator, I have found within me?

"Yet I am afraid even to rejoice—perhaps it is all self-deception. Perhaps in my rejoicing is hidden a sense of selfness and my Beloved will then leave me in disdain. Still! My heart is bursting, my soul is inflamed! My passion is burning and my divine service explodes in joy:

"Intimate Father! My soul is compelled to make a request, but help me!—I am afraid. Infinite worlds have You emanated from Your being—You have created, formed, and made them. Untold realms of spiritual beings have You created—awesome and fiery creations. Many great souls of saintly *tzaddikim* have You filled Your worlds with—each one in some way more saintly than the other. All are holy; all are pure; all are so great that we can conceive no proper name for their greatness. Yet they all stand ready to hallow themselves—to become more holy, more pure, and more great. With awe and with fear, with unceasing trepidation, they yearn to come closer to You. With the entire greatness of their beings and purity of their souls, they passionately yearn for You.

"But me? I just fall apart by the thought—I, who know myself, how shall I come close to You? Would this not be audacious of such a lowly creature as myself to request closeness to the infinite, awesome Creator? I feel paralyzed with shame; my limbs shiver with fear. But truthful God, please! There is nothing I can hide from You. What can escape Your omniscient knowledge? Everything is open for You. You see to the depths of my soul, to places where I myself cannot see. You know my deepest thoughts and desires, things that are unknown even to me. And from deep inside I feel so pressed. I cannot restrain from beseeching You.

"Father! My Master! Have mercy on me! Please pity my poor decrepit soul! Please calm my shaking soul and let me know if I am coming closer to You. Please let me know if the little good that is in me is Yours or, God forbid, mine: self-seeking and self-deception. To find out these answers is paramount in my life—if only I could know my soul's condition. Where is my soul holding now and what will be my eternal condition? Just give me permission and let my soul speak. Let me prostrate myself and beseech: 'Here is my soul, tormented and thirsting to surrender and melt in Your Presence. Here is my soul, beset to know if it has not detoured on its journey to You; a soul full of fear that instead of closeness, it has only distanced itself from You. Here is my soul, averse to life other than a life that is filled with You!'

"God! Light of my life! You are my only Treasure! When I feel Your holy Presence in me, my soul comes to life, but when You are hidden, my soul just withers!

A Silent Message
"But you earthly people, look well at the world—learn from it a lesson. Disperse to every corner to study

the grass and the trees, the great beasts and the wild animals: as long as they live, they grow and rejoice in life, but as they die, they shrivel and sadden. And if you are able, look to the heavens and see the seat of God's heavenly throne. Wherever you look, stars are twinkling—perhaps galaxies, planets, or comets. These bodies of light, mere reflections of Jewish souls, cast their mysterious light waves throughout all Creation. Why do their light waves seem to dance for joy, their rays gladden the heart of their beholder? But should a comet fall down to earth, it will lose all its sparkle and brilliance. Was this the body that once lit up the heavens and is now no more than a dull fallen stone?

"Explain to me, heavens or earth and their hosts, the secret of this riddle: what is the joy that seems to emanate from these heavenly and earthly bodies? Earthly creatures have their pains and discomforts, are hunted, fall prey, or just die. Why do their lives then seem so happy? Even blades of grass dance in the wind, expressing a celebration of life. Where does it come from, and why in their death do they seem so sad without knowing what death is about? Even without knowing that death is to come, beasts seem to sense its shadow with fear and sadness. Is it that they, too, have found some hidden treasure that keeps them happy while they are alive? Do they, like humans, mourn as their death approaches?

"Listen, earthly people, to the wrath of God's world directed toward people like you. A silent protest that your souls' ears can hear, listen to this message: 'Who is the shameful person who abandons his Creator to search for a treasure elsewhere? May the heavens and earth rage at him. Who is this shameless being who is brazen enough to walk in this world and to stand in the palace of God's servants while they sing: "God is our Treasure, our only possession; we have no desire but Him. We want only His will, to carry out His work, and to carve out the pathway to Him. We live in His light—that is our life's joy—and its absence is our death and sadness.'' '

"But deep even in your hearts, you earthly people, rumbles a great yearning for God. Like all of God's creatures you, too, seek your Creator, the ultimate meaning of your being, unbeknownst be this searching to you. But God passes you by, you cannot find Him, because you are not looking for Him. So to quench your souls' thirsting, to quell this incessant inner search, you transform the object of your search into 'gold.' You seek earthly treasures, illusory riches, which when attained you hope will fill your inner hole—like the mentally ill man who will pick up a stone and talk to it as if it were his deceased parent.

"The entire cosmos is the palace of God and its inhabitants all singers of God's praise. Never for a moment are they quiet; no movement do they let pass by—they praise God in all time and all space. Whether with might or with sound, with magnitude or minuteness, with radiance or with activity, even a leaf's rustle or the wind's whistle, they all are announcing the King: 'God is in all. His will rules all. Be awed by Him and praise His Name.'

The Secret of the Jew

"Therefore, Jewish People, how great is our lot! Though to others only a reflection of God's being appears, His very glory is deep within and all around us. God is the King Who reigns in His majesty, and we are His throne of glory—not only in spiritual worlds where the roots of our souls are, but even on this physical planet Earth. God's glory pervades all of Creation, and upon us Jewish People the King Himself sits.

"Does this surprise you, you Jewish person? Think, then, about this for a moment: are you sometimes not saddened, your soul perturbed, fearing you are from the lowliest of people? Do you feel that you are worse than those whose life-styles you yourself abhor, and do you find it difficult to encourage yourself? Do you catch yourself thinking, 'Who knows if there's still hope for me—is it still possible for me to heal my soul?'

"Where do these thoughts come from? What's all the rumble, if not the rumblings of your very own soul? Whence come these feelings of inadequacy if not from the soul's total surrender to God? And whence come the holy words you sometimes utter with fervor or the sudden insights into the secrets of God? They arise from God's Immanent Presence within you.

"So be silent now, universe. Hold back your song. Your exalted King must be coronated by me. Wait for the holy flame to be ignited by me, and only then will you be inflamed. As I lift up my voice, you follow suit, and together let us praise our God.

"As for you, gentile peoples, why do you oppress me and say, 'Where is your God Who dwells within you? We have yet to see Him Whom you claim is feared in all worlds; your claim of intimacy is yet to be seen.'

"But know, gentile peoples, God long knocks on our door: 'Open, dear children, the doors of your hearts. Open the gates of your very beings, and take Me into your hearts. My enemies stand ambush, they have burnt My Temple and razed My city and do not allow Me to enter. All that is holy to Me they seek to suppress, and all that is Mine they harass.'

"So since the destruction, we are God's secret palace. Our very beings are His holy fortress. Our bodies you can tread on, our bones you can burn, but

His Presence within us we shall guard—His Torah you are unable to touch.

"Therefore, our enemies, enemies of our God: do not revel or rejoice. God is with us—as intimate and as close as before. As in times long ago, His caresses still embrace us, but this only in the privacy of our souls. Sometimes He's so intimate, in the depths of our souls, that we ourselves can only sense His reflection.

"We are His temple, the fortress of God, though our bodies have been broken for His Name. Can you gentile people imagine our bliss? Such ecstasy of the soul have you known? I am beaten on my back before You, God, shamed to my face before You, dear Father. Chased and displaced, fleeced like a lamb, and all for Your holy Name. Intimate Father, God of the Jews! You are my only Treasure and possession!"

35

ILLNESS, RECOVERY, AND DEATH
OF THE REBBE'S SON

T he gall bladder stones that my son had
suffered from for several years became worse after the
summer of 5695 [1935]. From the Festival season onward, he hardly got out of bed. Then, on the 14th of
Kislev [December 10, 1935], we had to have him
brought urgently to the hospital accompanied by the
emergency first aid. His health deteriorated from day to
day until on the 12th of *Tevet* [January 7, 1936], we
were forced to operate. The operation was very difficult, but after a few days he started to improve. We
were optimistic that with God's help he would soon be
well. Then, on the 21st of *Tevet* [January 16], his
condition got worse again: blood was oozing from the
operation wound and it was impossible to stem it. We

feared for his life. After much effort, the doctors were, thank God, finally able to cut the flow, and he started to feel better again. But a few days later, the bleeding resumed and the doctors this time despaired. His appearance was really ghastly and the blood transfusions were not taking.

The doctors then said it was only a matter of hours, but praised be the Name of God, on the 28th of *Tevet* [January 23], he improved again. Then he came down with other illnesses, among them pneumonia, but miracle of miracles, God in His mercy cured him of these illnesses as well. Everyone, even the atheists, saw the greatness of God and were forced to believe and to praise Him.

In order to give praise and thanksgiving to God, even tokenly for all His great mercy on us, I have written the following memoirs. The metaphors I have used to depict the suffering we went through are not exaggerations at all. Rather, our suffering was so great that it seemed to take physical form in my eyes, and it is those forms that I am describing. Even the reference to "child," which I use here for my grown son, is out of the great pity we had for him in his bitter and helpless plight. So anything you see in these paragraphs that seem like just figures of speech are really accurate descriptions of my tangible feelings.

Dancing until Exhaustion

I raise my heart to the heavens, my prayer I sing to my God: "Please, God, how can I praise You? Please let me sing a song of my thanks for a millionth of the kindness You have bestowed on us. By day and by night, in every time of the year, my soul hums to sing thanks for Your great kindness—we did not deserve it.

I feel obliged to extol You, but in front of Your glory, I fear even to open my mouth.

"Please, God, accept now my deep desire to praise You, as You accepted the songs of the prophets. May the pulse of my yearning heart be as sweet in Your ears as was the music played by the Levites in the Temple.

"It is my duty, God, to dance in the streets, in the markets, in the ocean depths, and in the highest of clouds—even in Hell and with the stars. I shall sing and declare for all to praise You. Together we will extol Your Name. You have no beginning, nor have You an ending, and Your kindness to us is infinite.

"Why can I not express my heart's rumbling in song and the flames of my soul in tune? Enough that we cannot see the visions of the holy prophets, but why are our very own souls beyond our ken? Our spirits are storming like myriads of singing angels, yet we remain deaf to it all. Sweet songs of God are singing within us, yet we remain unaware of it all."

I repeat my prayer now: "Please, God, accept my deep desire to praise You, as You accepted the songs of the prophets. May the pulse of my yearning heart be as sweet in Your ears as was the music played by the Levites in the Temple.

"The entire world is Your rod to chastise us for our misdeeds, and each rod in Your merciful hand refines us. There is no existence besides Your great Being; nothing exists besides Your divine will. When You express wrath, the entire world would destroy us, but in Your mercy even Hell will embrace us. Blissful be the person who sees God's immanent hand and His rod he can recognize from afar. He thus repents of his misdeeds, hides his face, and cries: 'Please, God! I have sinned against You! Please, God, help me to never again betray You—let me devote the rest of my life to You! Save me now, God, and I shall serve You with all of my might! Strengthen my soul, God, and in thought, speech, and action I shall devoutly fulfill Your *mitzvot*! Have mercy on me, Father. Hide not Your Presence from me. Behold me and heal my soul.'

"A voice then is heard, the King's trumpets are declaring: 'God now is appeased with His servant.' There is no more nature. There is no more illness. There is nothing impossible, nor is there any lost case. The deathly ill become healed. Even the dying will come to life.

"All inhabitants of earth and creatures of the sea, all leaders of men sing to God; let all come hold hands and break out in dance, extolling the great Name of God. Every single being, from the smallest to the greatest, all come together and join hands. Together with the universe in a great cosmic dance, let us sing to the infinite and intimate God: 'You are all existence. Besides You there is nothing. You reign supreme and all happenings are Your work. This is our bliss, this is our lot, to sing for Your kindness to us. We dance before You for Your great love for us, singing to our last breath and dancing until exhaustion.'

Dread and Fear

"At the sight of Your rod, God, our souls nearly left us—those who saw us sighed and said: 'They are dead and gone from both worlds. Let them hope for death. May it come fast, and each day they wake up let them curse. Better that they should sleep forever and decay in the ground until no remnant of them is left. Their lives are not worth living, just pain upon suffering; their existence, strike after strike of God's rod.'

"But then, God, You revealed Your Presence and

brought us back to life in order to declare Your kindness and to serve You. May all those who see fate as inevitable be confounded and all those who trust nature be shamed. There is no nature, there is no illness, no impossibility, no lost case. God is the Master; He is all existence. He can do what He wants with His will. He brings life back to the dead, He heals the ill, and He makes life for the living pleasant.

"Please, God! How can I thank You? How can I sing praise for a millionth of Your kindness? What is my ability and what is my talent to praise You, Infinite One?

"You, God, are all existence—how dare we defile Your world? Everything that happens, You make it happen—how dare we defile Your doings? Yet in all that we do, our real desire is to serve You—this is our sacrifice. Even our speech, even our thoughts, are really meant to extol You—they are the limits of our expression of thanks.

"Please, God, have mercy! Bind us forever to our noble intentions. Help us carry out our holy yearnings—forever!

"But why, son, is your face so ghastly and ravaged, your appearance so dreadful and appalling—where is it from? The heart is melted to behold your hideous image, one's very being dissolves to see your gruesome face. The Infinite One must have sculptured His infinite wrath on your face.

"But now, God, have mercy and guide me with Your kindness—please stop tormenting me with Your wrath. Restrain Your wrath so that it will not distress me even in my imagination—I am very afraid of Your wrath. My heart contracts from the burden, my flesh shrivels when the thought of it comes to my mind. Like the roar of the predator in the ears of its prey as it sucks its blood and rips out its heart, so is the howling of Your agents of wrath as they pierce my ears and rend my soul. How frightful is Hell even after one escapes from it!

"Those fearsome nights! Those dreadful nights! For the rest of my life I shall tremble from their memory. And as long as I live I shall praise God, my Savior, Who redeemed me. In His infinite kindness He protected me from being devoured by those nights, and in His mercy He saved me from their fearful shadows—He held my shattered heart from disintegrating."

My Only Son!

Most of the lamps in the hospital had already gone out and the remainder were already very dim. Darkness, an oppressive darkness, now filled the room. It came down heavily on my entire being: my heart, my mind, and my entire body now felt so oppressed. I now could feel nothing, I could not even think—there was only the oppressive darkness.

So how can I just sit here as if I have such inner courage, after living through such a dreadful night? Several times today, my innards almost turned upside down. It was only God's hand that continued pumping my heart as the doctors and nurses toiled to restore my son's waning life—he was in a coma after the difficult operation. The dread has ground my bones to powder—how can I just sit here calmly?

And now the entire world has ceased to exist for me; I have lost all awareness of myself. All that exists, the focus of my whole life, is now only one thing: my son! My only son! He is deathly ill! He is being judged now in Heaven while here he fights for his life. He stands as if at the edge of the ocean, tossed back and forth between this world and the abyss.

I sit on the edge of his bed, dreading and trembling, my heart still shriveling, my breath almost choked. My son!

As I look down at your face now I can still catch some sign of life in the mumble of your white and exhausted lips. But who knows what will be after tomorrow, and even about tomorrow I'm not sure.

A Prayer You Will Answer

I banish these fearsome and dreadful thoughts from my mind. I force myself to have faith. Faith! Trust in God! I try to strengthen my spirits and my entire being with trust in God. As long as all is not over, we must strengthen ourselves in prayer and cry out to our merciful Father. I try, and with a trembling body, I beseech God:

"God! Merciful and benevolent! Since my childhood, my life has been full of pain. While still a young child, my enemies—worries and troubles—had already broken my strength and spirits. I was a little child when I was orphaned—I barely knew my father, the *tzaddik* that he was. I did not merit that my father, this holy and saintly man, should raise me.

"But God! Despite this I have no complaints or resentment toward You. You are righteous in all that You do, and if not for Your consistent kindness throughout my troubles, I would surely have been lost in my sorrows. Please, God! You have delivered me from all my suffering. Now, too, have mercy on me for the sake of Your great Name and in the merit of my holy ancestors.

"Have pity, please, God, on my downtrodden soul—stop breaking our already broken hearts! Have mercy on us, compassionate Father, and please heal our son! Have compassion on us and grant us a gift: our only son, the fat of our souls. But I question myself, saying: 'Do I desire and pray for his healing only because he is ours?' 'No,' I answer myself. 'The actual pain of this boy—his pain is what so distresses me.'

"God! Look at the pitiful way he just lies in bed. Look at his ghastly complexion. Have pity on this poor soul, who is now in such suffering and pain."

I continue to pray to God, to pour out my soul before Him. I would like to pray such a prayer in which I will feel that God has heard my voice and already saved me. Once, during a previous predicament, I did experience this, but this time I don't seem able to. My heart is closed, and I cannot offer a passionate prayer.

"God! Show me how to pray so that my deliverance will be assured. As long as he still breathes, have mercy on me. . . . Help me to offer an earnest and fervent prayer that will be assured of Your answer."

Faith beyond Destruction

My whole body shivers and I am covered with sweat; I would tear off my skin if I could. Who knows if tomorrow there will be anything to hope and pray for. Now I still hope, but my prayer seems shut out. I run in front of the King's gate to shout, but lo, the gate is closed. From here I am taken and thrown into the pit of Hell; its gate has been closed behind me. Everything is locked up, my prayer has been silenced. Who knows if it will not, God forbid, be too late.

I look again at the child. Is it movement or, God forbid, the throes of death? His condition is worsening, his breathing heavier—my entire being trembles and disintegrates. My heart feels as if some hand is squeezing it without mercy—just squeeze a little harder and my heart will stop.

I feel that ounce after ounce of strength is leaving

me; my entire existence is ceasing to be, as if I am slipping below the threshold of humanness, of the entire human world. Even that which I still can discern is not a human discerning. Yet that which is beyond human discerning, I seem able to sense.

And now, outside, a storm is raging. Thunder! A torrent rain that could douse the sun pours upon us. Is God spewing upon us all His phlegm that the rain seems to be striking just upon us? From all directions, the lightning seems to be striking just us. Roaring thunder. Shock. Destruction. Like a soldier fallen in battle, my entire body is shriveled, sprawled on the ground.

Again, I try to encourage myself and my faith. I am sure that the infinite God, He and only He, can deliver me from the abyss of my bitter sorrows. But there is no self left within me to encourage, no spirit left to lift up. I am entirely broken—my broken bones have been crushed to dust.

And such glaring images about our dreadful future spontaneously appear before me: what will *Shabbat* look like? What about Pesach? My entire life looks like sorrow and pain. How can I live a life like this?

I offer vows—not just financial ones, but I offer my very self: to rectify my soul and thus, please God, to improve my lot.

A Song for a Vision

"There is no holiness like that of our God; there is no source of mercy besides Him.

"All inhabitants of earth nullify your deified ego-selves before the glory of God's greatness. And the internal images of earthly passions that you worship, subdue them to His royal rule. If you seek Him, His immanence will enlighten you. If you follow His ways, He will bring you success.

"Lofty and exalted Creator! You have looked down from the heavens into Hell and seen me pathetically shriveled up in its abyss. Eternal Being! From Your majestic palace You have descended to my downtrodden and abject soul, and in the nick of time You have rushed to save me. You showed me from afar Your desire to save me and in so doing, You restored my spirits."

Suddenly I envisioned sitting at *Shalosh Seudos* and next to me sat my son. I was deeply moved and shaken by this image. In the darkness of Hell, under such oppression—I and my whole world were being devoured by flame and smoke—such a beautiful vision that I could barely hope for could not have come from my own conscious thought. Such an encouraging picture of salvation could not have arisen from my own will. "God! It was You Who had mercy on me and shined a ray of hope to my beaten soul."

I am deeply shaken, almost in trance: there in my vision I want to take my son's hand, just to hold it and to kiss it . . . but then I am taken aback. Should I not rather rejoice in God who saved us, to prostrate my entire body before Him? Would it not be more proper to praise and extol Him for the boundless kindness that He bestowed?

"Please, God! You are infinite, Your power is limitless. When You smite us with Your powerful hand, we cannot bear it, but neither can we bear being lifted too swiftly from Hell to bliss. Before my eyes lies my dying child, but in my vision I see him sitting next to me at *Shalosh Seudos* in perfect health."

I became roused to sing praise to God, but words remained beyond me. I feel there's a stormy sea within me whose waves just toss me toward God, to praise Him and to extol His Name, but I know no words that can convey my tidal waves of emotion. "You have bestowed on us kindness beyond our capability to receive—I am incapable even to thank You. Your salvation is beyond our capacity to conceive. We have no concept how to even start to praise You." God had chastised me, and I felt the blow—my very self almost ceased to exist. Even my feelings of gratitude were almost beyond human limits to sustain. The thanks to God that I now feel, I myself cannot conceive. The song of my soul to the Master of souls cannot be contained in the words I have sung, nor can my own thoughts even grasp it.

Chaos and Confusion

"I shall extol You, God, My Father and Master, for all the great things You did for us. You chose us to be Your vehicle of revelation through which to reveal Your power. You chastised us, purged us, and refined us. You strengthened faith in your power in our hearts and in the hearts of others. We all saw and recognized that there is none like our God, our Creator, our Leader, our Savior.

"You made us like a ball tossed back and forth in play between the hands of Your heavenly agents. When the agent of bliss received us in his hands, we were relieved, thinking that we were saved. The child is better, his strength is coming back, so we rejoiced and passed on the good news. 'He is ours!' we all said as he recovered."

Then suddenly we were tossed to the agent of Hell and found ourselves in greater danger than before. His life was gushing out together with his blood; the strongest medicines were unable to stop it. Even the efforts of the most skilled doctors were futile and ineffective. They then gave up all hope for restoring his poor soul, which ebbed out together with his blood. All our hopes were in vain and our efforts useless. One of the doctors even refused to answer our questions about the condition of our dear, suffering child.

But a second doctor had pity on my family's plight. He rallied me to brace myself in order to save them from emotional breakdown when the time, God forbid, would come. "How great is Your power, God, that You braced me and kept the light of my spirits from going out!"

Then my family began to scream, wailing at the top of their lungs—they thought he was already dead. Chaos and confusion, our bodies were numbed. Only embittered spirits were left. Dark and embittered, tossed back and forth, our spirits writhed in pain and blood.

No Laws of Nature

"But there is none like You, God, nothing like Your mercy! Our cries and bloody tears that poured like water, together with those of our family and friends, You accepted and annulled the decree. Even the curtain between my heart and the gates of Your Heaven You tore open—You lit up the heavy darkness in my heart with a flash of light. I then felt sure that You would save us, and I was deeply shaken. This was the prayer that I had hoped for: 'Blessed be You, God, the merciful, for Your salvation. Blissful is he who has faith in You and who pours out his soul to You in prayer.'

"You are so great, God, Your limitlessness is beyond comprehension. We are so trifling and insignificant before You, and even this we only at times can see. My spirits are so weak that even when You shined this ray of hope and salvation into my heart, my spirits were unable to sustain it. So when waves of wrath again engulfed me, when oppressive mountains with their weight again crushed me, when the doctors were saying the hours were numbered, I questioned the voice of hope in my heart—how can I know it's not just delusion. If the child's voice, which was only like the coo of a dove, can now almost not be heard, who can vouch that my heart's wishes are not deceiving me?

"Creator of all existence! You created countless worlds and creatures out of nothing! As You have done in the past, You once again opened the heavens to reveal Your might and Your power. You thus smash all of mankind's illusions, saying: 'All inhabitants of earth, see that only I rule the world and beside Me there is no power. There are no laws of nature or any rules that are beyond My jurisdiction. If it is good things that you hope for, it is Me you must hope to. If it is misfortune that you fear, it is only Me you must fear. All that exists only proclaims My existence—whatever angels do in Heaven or worms on earth—is all My doing.' Blessed are You, God, blessed is Your Name. You have healed our son beyond the laws of nature and beyond human comprehension.

"By day and by night, in every season and occasion, my soul yearns to sing of Your magnanimous kindness. You expect this from me, but I am too awed to open my mouth. Please, God! Besides my soul, I have nothing! This soul of mine I wish to offer to You. Please, Father, I beg You, my Master: do not shame me and refuse my offer.

"Merciful God, please help me for the rest of my life: may all my thoughts, my actions, and even my breathing be to manifest the greatness of Your Name. Remove all obstacles from my path, both inner and outer blocks. Save Your People, and us among them, on all levels of our physical and spiritual lives. Draw us closer—we surrender to You! Help us to serve You with joy and sincerity with every aspect of our deepest selves!''

My Son—Where Are You?

Now I sit still and silent. The intensity of pain is beyond bearing—I am broken beyond repair. After receiving God's gracious gift, our dear and beloved son, a sincere and outstanding Torah scholar, wise and straightforward, noble and refined, deeply attached to me at the soul level (he would have been ready to sacrifice his life for me), after God saw our dire plight and returned us this dear gift by healing our son from his serious illness, it was decreed in Heaven a harsh decree, a very bitter one, to take him from from me in 5700 [1939] at the outbreak of the war. On the 12th of *Tishrei* [October 7,] during the bombing, he was mortally wounded—he was standing near me. A few days later, on the second day of Sukkot, the 16th of *Tishrei* [October 11], he returned his pure and holy soul to his Maker.

Also at that time, my daughter-in-law, his wife, was killed while standing outside the hospital. That was on the 13th of *Tishrei* [October 8]. Her name was Gittel, daughter of Rabbi Shlomo Chaim of Balichav. All hope for myself and my soul both in this world and the next was aborted with their premature deaths. And my own future in them through their continued spiritual growth was also destroyed for me. The tragedy is too great to bear—only You, God, can sustain and encourage me with Your wonders.

"Kindness is Yours, God, and the shame is mine—my own misdeeds have brought this on me. Compassionate Father, You know the heart of a father toward his beloved son. Who besides You knows how broken my heart is, how crushed is my very being? Nevertheless, I now take courage to thank You for this precious gift You gave us. You even added nearly four full years to his life after his illness. I praise You and extol You for this beloved treasure that You gave us for thirty-one years. How happy I was then—the sun's rays dimmed in my eyes compared to the pure shine I saw in his face.

"Please, God, have pity on a poor Jew like me. Have mercy on me, Father and Master! Listen to the petition of my heart, which wallows in pain and sorrow.

"All the time I had Your precious gift, my son, I watched over him with all my might. With my heart and my soul and with Your help, I protected him from all harm. My very own life was for me second to his. But now I am haunted by the thought, 'Where is my son? I need to watch him. For his delicate body I was ready to sacrifice my life—now, where is he?'

"My soul trembles greatly. What can I do for my son, dearer to me than my own life? I must do something to protect him from harm—even from worry and fear. My soul is exhausted from finding a way to do something to help him in some way. God! Protector of the Jewish People! Protect our son, Elimelekh Ben-Tzion, and his wife, Gittel, whom You have taken to You. May their righteousness always shine before You, may my prayers for them always find favor in Your eyes. Bring them closer to You, merciful God. Grant them bliss and all of Your goodness. Always raise them higher, even beyond their righteousness and beyond my prayers for them.

"Store their souls in the source of all life and may You, God, be their inheritance. May they rest in peace in their repose.

"Master of the Universe! Call a stop to our suffering! May these dear departed souls, together with all the past suffering of the deceased and the living, atone for all our sins.

"Have mercy from now on, God, on each of us and on the Jewish People—grant us only good things from now on. May I myself be included with all my family and friends among the Jewish People to receive Your kindness. Grant us right now the eternal redemption, rebirth of the dead, and a complete physical and spiritual salvation. Amen."

36

PERSONAL SONG

A person must build for himself ladders upon which to ascend to Heaven. Song, a *niggun*, is one of those ladders, especially when sung after the joy of a *mitzvah* and with a humble heart.

Every person has a unique portion in the "World of Melody," so when singing, turn up the sound of your personal song. If you do not tune in to that personal melody but just sing someone else's song, you are just swallowing someone else's saliva.

37

A SILENT CRY TO GOD

One should be able to speak to God not only in speech but even more so in thought—and in thought that comes from deep within. "I call out to You, God, from the depths" (Psalm 130:1). On the conscious, superficial levels of my soul, I know nothing; the depths of my soul cry out for themselves.

"God! You are so immanent yet at the same time so transcendent. Our yearning is very strong but our capability is very weak. God! You bring us closer with Your infinite power!"

38

PERSONAL RULES FOR
SPIRITUAL GROWTH—II

If you have been able to compile relevant maxims and personal rules for your spiritual growth, wonderful! But if not, it shows that you have not devoted yourself and your life to growing, or, that you are some sort of being without a personal identity.

Because whoever dedicates his life to spiritual progress will inevitably be confronted by difficulties and impediments. These will not only be external, such as making a livelihood, but also internal blocks: indolence, negative tendencies, destructive character traits, and so forth. Someone who is constantly involved in the inner struggle for self-improvement sometimes wins and sometimes loses. From experience, conclusions can be drawn: when you do this, you win; when you do that, you lose.

Since no two people are alike in character and tendencies, and the inner struggles, successes, and failures of each are not the same, each person must draw up his own guidelines and self-advice, which will be different from any other's, each tailored for his own unique inner experience.

So if one has not come up with his own guidebook to the spiritual life, it is either because he has not dedicated his life to struggling for self-improvement (in which case he knows of neither loss nor gain) or he is some anonymous being, so unaware of his own self that he cannot identify his unique inner struggle—the purpose of his being.

39

THE VALUE OF TIME

I recently visited a rich man who earns his living with minimum toil—he doesn't even have to leave his house. Other worries I also did not find in his life: he is physically healthy and emotionally he feels content.

But one thing I noticed did bother him: how should he spend all his free time? To solve this, he would just sit and chat with his wife and family to alleviate his boredom. He thus seemed to me to be like the poor soul who was granted entrance to *Gan Eden* because while on earth he had saved two Jewish lives from death. But because he was an ignorant wagon driver who had no grasp of what *Gan Eden* is all about, he was placed in a beautiful palace and handed a whip that he could wave to his heart's desire. The angels finally had compassion on him that he was forfeiting *Gan Eden* with his whip. I heard this story from my father-in-law o.b.m.

So I, too, had compassion on this poor rich man who has so much free time—every minute could be a *Gan Eden*. How much could he accomplish with this time? In a day? A week? A lifetime? . . . And he squandered it on idle chatter.

And I was so jealous of his free time. If only he could bequeath me four hours a day so that I could have twenty-eight hours, how much happier we both would be. He would be freed of the burden of four boring hours, while I would come into the fortune of this *Gan Eden*.

But why should I envy his time, such idle time, such an empty and barren existence, which has no meaning or content? He does not enjoy the triumphs that follow the setbacks so inherent to the spiritual life—his whole life revolves around the pleasure he gets out of eating. Would my soul not abhor to receive such barren and empty hours?

So why do I look at his spare time and not look at my own? Can I myself not cut down on my hours of sleep, can I not find here and there some free moments? These wasted minutes that pass unnoticed—can I not somehow condense them together into one set period and use it for spiritual progress?

If you are willing to exert yourself, you will find storehouses of hidden time.

40

THE ULTIMATE DETERRENT
TO SIN

here is no better deterrent with which to rein in your baser urges than the deterrent of your own emotional response: the regret and soul-deep anguish that will torment you after you fall into sin. This is more than sufficient to quiet your urges and to steer clear of any undesirable behavior.

But there remains a problem with this: even at the peak of your regret and anguish, your baser urges are still alive within you. Deep down there, inside, they are even then preparing their next plan of mischief. Because of this, the very action you regret will be down-played in your eyes, and your anguish will be diminished. You will even become angry with yourself for being upset and will try to suppress those positive feelings.

For this reason our Sages advised in order to overcome your baser urges, "Remember the day of your death" (*Berakhot* 5a). They were specific in saying the "day" of your death and not just your death, because *on that day even before you die* your baser urges terminate.

Then, with these distorting lenses removed, you will see the true repulsiveness of those baser urges. Your entire life will then pass through your memory as if it were just a few hours, full of all your baser behavior. Even the few good things you did throughout your lifetime will pass by almost unnoticed because they were so few and far between. And then . . . how deep will be your torment!

"Why did I do that for no benefit or good reason? Why did I misuse my only lifetime as a descent to unholy depths? My soul will soon fall into the abyss of Hell, accompanied by the demonic beings waiting even now around my deathbed to receive me. Why didn't I use my lifetime to draw close to God, to turn back to the arms of my Father with a holy and purified soul?"

Then you will want to slash your heart, to lacerate your soul out of anguish. This is deep soul-regret. That is why we say, "Remember the day of your death." And further, this very base act that you now contemplate will pass through your memory on your last day if you do it. Then, how much will you regret having done it? How much torment and anguish will you have? So bring that undesired future experience into the present as a deterrent to baser behavior.

41

LOATHING YOUR BASER URGES—II

ou cannot release yourself from your baser urges unless you loathe them as well. Develop abhorrence toward your urges—they can destroy both your earthly and eternal worlds by clouding your thinking and your emotions.

By developing this hatred for your baser urges, it will be easier for you to subdue them. There will be times that the only way you will be able to control your urges will be with the ability to find them disgusting, like the urge for immoral acts that are so sensually tempting.

42

A PRAYER FOR EFFICIENT LIFE

Master of the Universe! How much longer do I have yet to live? When will I be able to fulfill my life's mission: to bring out the books of spiritual guidance, insights, and interpretations that lie in the depths of my soul? Would seventy, eighty, or even ninety years of continuous effort be sufficient to realize my life's dream and desire?

"Please, God! Grant me yet many years! Bless my limited time with efficient and productive endeavors: may every stroke of my pen convey multiple ideas."

When King David beseeched God, "Please don't take me away in half my days" (Psalm 102:25), he meant not just half the number of days but rather half their quality in efficiency—I should be able to realize my potential, my life's mission.

43

APPROACHING THE GRAVE

ortal man! Don't you realize that you are constantly leaving this world? With every action, with every breath, you are nearing your death and your grave. Why do you delude yourself into thinking that you can settle down forever in this world? Then in your last 'step' on earth, when you are being lowered into the grave, then you will shout, 'Dear earthly world, why do you leave me? Who has brought me down to here?' ''

King Shlomo referred to this when he said, ''Its steps bring one near to the grave'' (Proverbs 5:5): every step a person takes in this world is a step closer to the grave.

44

GETTING BEYOND ULTERIOR MOTIVES

If you want your learning for personal gain to bring you to learning with pure intentions, then delve deeply into your Torah learning. Gather every ounce of mind power you have and concentrate on in-depth Torah learning. If your learning, though for personal gain, is not in this way, it is unlikely you will ever reach pure intention.

This is because the difficulty of reaching pure intention in learning is due to the human soul's in-grained nature of doing things only for its own benefit: all desires and thoughts revolve around self-fulfillment. Therefore, even if you want to learn with pure intentions, the desire for personal gain enters your mind, contaminating the pure intention with personal, ulterior motivations.

And what is this "pure" intention itself? A simple, formless life-drive. This drive is vital to the human being. Take for instance the sensation of hunger—this alone is not enough to drive a person to eat. If someone doesn't have a desire to live, he will not prepare meals, he will not earn a living to provide for his meals, and he may not eat at all. We see this in depressed people. Even when they are hungry, they do not eat because they have little desire to live. All the much more so, they have no interest in procreation—they don't want to perpetuate life.

So God instilled in us a simple drive for life: one undifferentiated drive and not many. We have no separate desire to eat, to drink, and so forth. Rather we have a simple drive to fill all that we lack. Whatever you want at any specific moment will become the objective of your simple drive.

This force is like a stormy ocean: here waves are rising to sink a ship, there, to drown a beast. But also valueless items and even rubbish are devoured by the waves, anything that falls in their path. There are no different waves, some hungry for ships, some for beasts, others for even rubbish. Just one storm, one ocean, which appears in different places and devours different things. The same is true of a human being: after you have allayed your hunger pains and are full, your drive is channeled to quench your thirst.

But this aimless drive, when it has nowhere to go, will crave useless things as well. I have seen this happen with elderly people who now have nothing with which to fill their lives: they are driven to play at childish pastimes as if they were children themselves. Their simple, formless drive that accompanied them throughout their lives was misdirected, and they have become habituated to filling their lives with empty things. They are like the ocean waves, driven blindly by the storm to useless pursuits.

So even if a person occasionally learns with pure intention, as long as he has not channeled this primal life energy away from objectives of personal ego gain, it will always be redirected back toward personal gain. Torah learning will remain just another means for personal advancement because this is the natural outlet for the drive in the person.

However, if you submerge your drive for personal gain into in-depth Torah learning, eventually such learning arouses a love for the actual learning. Soon you will be so involved in the depths of your learning that you will have totally forgotten about your original intention. Now, the very learning is what concerns you: each point that you don't understand really bothers you, each new point of knowledge elates you. And to the degree that you delve deeper into your studies, to that degree your pure, aimless life-force is directed into your learning. Then, when the objectives of personal gain have disappeared into the depths of Torah learning, the pure, selfless drive can shine forth untainted by any ulterior motives.

45

DISSOLVING THE EGO–SELF

And I stand between God and you" (Deuteronomy 5:5). The Baal Shem Tov explained this to mean that the "I"—the ego, the sense of selfness that we feel and that drives us to seek only our own selfish needs—is what stands between God and one's true self—the soul.

But how do we get past the barrier imposed by the ego–self? Only by mutually nurturing relations with other human beings—you cannot do it by yourself. This is also alluded to in the verse "And I stand"—when I stand by myself, then there is the barrier "between God and man."

Now the dynamics of experiencing oneself so intensely—to the point that all senses, emotions, and

desires revolve around providing only for this self—
seems to be a psychological, ego defense system. This
develops as we grow and unconsciously perceive how
everybody else is just out for himself, something that
makes us feel alone and abandoned in the world. "Who
will care for me if I don't stand up for myself?" So this
lonely self learns to strengthen its defenses in order to
provide for itself. Gradually, a thick protective shell of
selfishness grows around it: the I, the me, the myself,
besides which there is nothing else.

Maybe for this reason women and children are
more compassionate toward others, more so than adult
men. They basically have someone who cares and
provides for them: a husband for his wife and parents
for their children. Not feeling abandoned in this world,
they have no need to build a protective shield around
the self. And because their sense of selfness has not been
blown out of proportion, they are more able to see
through to the predicament of others and to have
compassion for them.

Creating the Ideal Society

So the way to minimize and even dissolve this "I,"
this selfishness that separates you from God, is to seek
out close friendships with like-minded spiritual seekers.
Each one should be as concerned about the other's
welfare as his own. Share each other's worries and joys,
help and guide each other on the spiritual path. Eventually the feeling of loneliness and abandonment will
disappear, and it will be easier to uproot this self-
seeking from within you.

Do not misunderstand this to mean the communal
society system espoused by secular scholars. It is the
Sefer HaIkkarim, I believe, who quotes Aristotle as
saying that the ideal society is where everything is

commonly owned: business, wealth, everything—one common bank account. But these secular scholars could only grasp the seeming separateness of the material world—they could not see beyond it. They had no idea of the essential oneness of all human souls. So in order to bridge what they saw as the gap of separate human beings, the Aristotelian school proposed communal living. But this does not solve their problem, because on the physical level a human being is an inherent separate entity—he can never be merged with another. Furthermore, the secular system fails to heal the wounds of the human spirit and soul, which are encapsulated within human bodies and therefore experience their separateness. Hence, the human spirit remains trapped in its earthly shell, seeking only to gratify the self with sensual pleasures, resenting those who in any way scratch the shell of the self, and reveling in self-pride. And all these baser behaviors are done in the name of "equality" behind the false facade of communal living. The *Sefer HaIkkarim* quotes the description of this "ideal" society where people "share" each other's wives and "share" possessions, commonly known as adultery and robbery. All this is done under the flag of communalism.

But the Torah way is different. Each person retains his wealth and all other personal belongings. It is only the soul that transcends separateness and becomes shared, not selfish—sharing desires, worries, and joys with others. He also wishes that his friends should have the blessings he does, and if his friend needs a favor, he will promptly do it. All this brings a person to feel that his life has a purpose that transcends his own small self and he belongs to humanity. This then enables us to uproot the selfishness from our hearts and to reach up toward God—together.

46

BLIPS OF SUPERCONSCIOUSNESS

 Jewish person should be able to rise above his own level. There should be times at which you feel such an inspiration and uplifting that you yourself do not know what you are experiencing. You may even say things at these times that will take you years to understand.

47

SHALOSH SEUDOS: THE WEEKLY YOM KIPPUR—II

halosh Seudos time on Shabbat—the weekly Yom Kippur. Just as Yom Kippur reveals the soul and purifies it from a year of alienation, so too does the Shalosh Seudos bring out the yearnings and anguish of the soul that were hidden throughout the week. During the week, the soul strives for the heights. It struggles with its inner evil and with the needs of the body and other distractions. These so trample upon it that sometimes its very voice is silenced. A person forgets he even has a soul that yearns for God.

But then comes Shalosh Seudos, a time when a Jew is able to leave behind the entire world, to draw near to God and communicate with Him. Now, all the soul's torment and yearnings that were silenced throughout the week are able to be expressed. One minute you feel a passionate yearning—when you sing, "Draw Your servant near to Your will"; the next minute you feel deeply heartbroken: "God! Please! Heal my soul!" And if then you pay attention to the cries of your soul, you will hear the voice of a kidnapped princess, struggling to escape from the rogues who have attacked her. She yearns to return to the palace of her father: "Father! Father! Save me from these rogues and return me to You!"

48

TALKING TO CREATION

otza'ei Shabbat, the First Selichot 5689 [1929].

I am exhausted from talking to people about God. I am constantly trying to convey how God is so immanent right in front of us, even within us, in our thoughts and our actions. God fills our entire outer and inner worlds, our deepest recesses and all our life experiences.

But all people see is the earthly world, and they bury their heads in it with their entire beings. If only they would listen to my cries: "Follow the voice of God in all your physical and spiritual actions—your entire life is in His Presence." But they have blinded themselves with their physical perceptions, and their hearts sense nothing beyond their physical senses.

My throat is hoarse. Fresh ideas about how to convey these truths are not forthcoming. The sharp insights I've had in the past are dimming—I feel about to fall into depression, God help me.

When I had left the Friday night *Shabbat* table I gave up—no one had been listening anyway. So I began to talk to the universe. I opened my window and I saw an entire world just waiting for someone to acknowledge its beauty. I was then about to recite the bedtime *Keriyat Shema*, so I spoke to the world and cried out to it: "*Shema Yisrael* . . . God is One!"

I continued reciting: "Enlighten the world with Your glory . . . . Blessed be God by day, blessed is He by night. . . . *Adon Olam*, Master of the Universe Who reigned before Creation. . . .When all came into being through His will, then He was called the Ultimate King. . . ." The entire Creation seemed to be taking in each holy word and thought as I expressed it. I became greatly encouraged and all my insights and feelings returned to me.

Now, whether by myself or with people, whether or not anyone is listening, I speak instead to the world, to God's world, rather than to people.

. . . And when the world itself will reveal its holiness, perhaps then also its inhabitants will become hallowed with it. Then, from the far corners of the earth, songs to God will they all be singing.

APPENDIX A

THE IMPORTANCE OF
SELF-KNOWLEDGE

t is futile to think that somewhere there is some panacea prescription to heal the human soul. There is no such thing. Each person must write his own—by honest self-awareness of the intricacies of his unique soul.

The Rambam (Maimonides) writes in the first of "The Eight Chapters" (his introduction to *Pirkei Avot*) that sickness of the soul requires a spiritual healer no less than a physical ailment needs a doctor. He writes that just as the latter must first know the entire system of the human body and the dynamics of all its parts in order to effect a cure, so too must the spiritual healer know the entire human spiritual system and the dynamics of all parts of the soul. He does not mean

knowledge only of the really sick soul and its patholog-
ical patterns but also knowledge of the healthy soul: its
emotions, its motives, and its fears. Then the healer will
know how to work *with* the soul, to make proper use of
the human body and animal soul and transform them
both into faithful servants of the higher soul—not only
occasionally during times of spiritual service but as a
permanent condition as well.

In the *Noam Elimelekh* (*VaEtchanan*, q.v. *His-
hamer Lekha*), we find an astounding thought on this
matter. He says there that it is impossible for a person to
maintain consciousness of God's eminence and greatness unless he first delves into the essence of his own
soul. This is because the soul is similar to God in five
ways. If one has no insight into knowledge of his own
soul, he can have no insight into its source, the Creator.
He is saying that not only for one's elementary spiritual
health does one need to know himself in order to be
able to work with the dynamics of his soul but also to
attain higher spiritual levels and closeness to God one
must have deep self-knowledge.

But one of the major points to keep in mind when
studying the soul is that it differs from how God
interrelates with Creation. Though the soul fills the
body as God fills the world, God is not in any way
limited or contained within it. Neither is He affected or
influenced by it. The human soul, however, is intimately bound up with and influenced by the human
body and animal soul.

This is one of the reasons people are different.
Besides the fact that the actual makeup of each person's
soul is different, the effect of the body on the soul also
is crucial. If a person's physiological, neurological, and
cardiological systems are more refined and efficient,
then also the soul that is contained within them will be

affected for the better. But if these systems are more gross, then the soul also will become grosser. Because of this, even in a single person there will be differences not only in his behavior but also in his soul condition, depending upon his physical state.

Even further, one's soul condition when he lived a wanton life is not like that when he becomes a religious person. And even if he were always a religious person, his soul condition prior to dedicating his whole being to the spiritual life is not like what it will be when he does. And how great is the difference between generations, besides the inherent difference in their actual souls? The changing modes of behavior and life-styles, of language, manners of speech, and accepted thought have their effect upon the generations and create a gap between them.

This is why the Rambam, more so than previous ethical works, stressed self-knowledge—because the change in soul conditions of his generation required new understandings and insight. What shall we say, then, in our generation when both our physical and spiritual conditions have so drastically changed? In order to restrain its energies and tendencies from flowing to baser outlets and redirect them in the service of God, in order to use our self-knowledge as a means to attain some knowledge of God, we must dive to the depths of our own souls to discover how they are in the here and now.

We are not advising anyone to study pathology of the soul and to become a psychiatrist like those in the world today. How incomparable is their path to ours and their knowledge to what we know! This is because of a well-known fact: knowledge of the nature of the workings of the mind, the emotions, and all other psychological functions is possible only by personal experience—one must discover them in himself empirically. One must look deep within his own soul and listen to whispers of his heart. Then, comparing discoveries with others who have done the same will also be of great help. Studying the subtleties and elusiveness of the mind and the soul is unlike studying the physical body. The body is right there—you can touch it, scrutinize it, and even dissect someone else's dead body. But you cannot do that with a soul—its thoughts and feelings are invisible to an outsider. So in the end, everyone must be his own analyst.

Now today's secular psychologists are, in general, people without Torah values: there are behaviors that in their minds are not censurable and perhaps even to be admired, whereas a religious Jewish person abhors the very idea of them, let alone the action. So all these people find in human nature is what they look for because it interests them: vulgar thoughts and filthy fantasies. For this reason, not only are our thought processes and content so different from theirs but also our souls are incomparable. And again, this is besides the fact of the Jewish soul's higher divine nature, but because our respective souls have been affected by what we respectively think about. Even they admit that the soul is affected by one's thoughts to the point that there are many nervous disorders that are not neurological or brain dysfunctional in origin but rather psychosomatic: they were caused by the sordid thoughts and desires that the individual became addicted to.

So because these analysts have studied only the type of soul that for thousands of years has been molded by a material life-style and thoughts void of Torah and spiritual values, they perceive the human soul as a den of evil spirits and assume that man is doomed a prisoner to these shadowy forces.

This is not the case with us, God's Chosen People.

For over three thousand years, intimacy with God has been our passion. His holy Torah and beautiful *mitzvot* have filled our minds with thought. Some devote themselves to this life more than others, but all of us—our young, our aged, our children, and our wives—have set seeking God as the ultimate objective of our thoughts. How many prophets, sages, mystics, and saints has God sent over the ages to sanctify us in thought and in action. Especially so is the path of the Baal Shem Tov. Its main goal is to refine the lower soul and even the physical body with a sense of the forthcoming sanctity in the ultimate transformation of the future.

Can you, then, compare our souls, our bodies, our thoughts, traits, emotions, and deepest feelings to those whose lives are so completely different? If there are those among today's psychologists who feel in a position to denigrate the human soul, it is only because they themselves are looking at the spiritual dunghill of a decadent humanoid being—the filthy thoughts and indecent desires to which they also are privy. Even the spark of divinity that lies at the core of their being has been concealed by this inner garbage and thus has been barred entry into their conscious awareness.

As for us, even our lower soul is holy. This soul, together with all the pathways with which it expresses itself in our being, is what we want with God's help to uncover. Each person must attain self-knowledge and know how to master his inner life.

The conclusions for self-guidance that will arise from this study are of utmost importance and value to us. With them we will be able to channel all our bodies' energies, our tendencies, and our thoughts to God as a permanent soul-condition. It is not enough to be just a "religious Jew"—make yourself into a deeply spiritual person.

APPENDIX B

LEVELS OF FREE WILL

ll the worlds and all that is in them, even their most material substances, are all only rays of divineness. Each one shines with a unique brilliance and an intensity of its own: the higher worlds, way beyond ours and our comprehension, and our world in its own manner and fashion. Nevertheless, the root of the Jewish soul transcends them all, being intimately bound with God and His will. Even further, all the worlds can be enlightened only via the Jewish soul because, while they receive only a reflection of divine illumination, the Jewish soul is enlightened by the actual light.[1]

---

[1]An illumination is not the actual light at its source, just a reflected ray. The light at a candle's flame is the actual light, but the

This explains why only the Jewish person has absolute free choice, something no other earthly or heavenly being has. What is free choice? A will of which the person himself is the absolute author. The primal cause of soil to give forth what is planted in it is not the soil itself—the process does not begin in the soil. There must be rain to bring out the soil's powers and, before that, there must be clouds to bring the rain. Each thing is brought about by a prior factor.

Even the will that an animal exhibits in moving from place to place does not originate in the animal but in the grass that it sees out there—it is the *grass* that triggers the animal's will. The animal is compelled by the grass and can do nothing but go to it.

Ultimately it is God Who is the Cause of all causes and Author of all factors, compelling everything to do His will. The sun will rise, causing the weather to change, causing rain to fall, causing things to grow, each thing in a sequence. This person will prosper because of a specific factor or, God forbid, suffer through a specific cause. Someone else will get ill, whether a condition that arises from the person himself or whether he goes somewhere and is infected by a certain person with a contagious illness, and the same when he recuperates. It is all brought about by various causes and factors. But the ultimate cause is God's

---

light in the house is only a reflection of it. And then there is a reflection of the reflection: if the room where the candle sits is open to another room and the door is not opposite the candle, then the light that enters the second room is not the candle's prime illumination but only a reflection of the light in the first room. This subsidiary reflection of the candle's illumination or reflected light is of course less intense than that of the candle's own light in the first room.

spontaneous and independent will. He has absolutely no external influences, just His will. God created the world simply because He wanted to, and this is how He continues to sustain it. God is always recreating the universe each day, every moment, and guiding it according to His will.

So if God dictates all that happens, then there is nothing in Creation with absolute free will—free of any external cause. As in our previous example, an animal has absolutely no will that we can say originates in the animal. The animal does not want because *it* wants but is compelled by external forces. The grass that it sees sparks its preprogrammed will to want to eat that grass. Its will is not self-initiated.

But a human being has the potential to exercise absolute free will, not only to decide what he does or doesn't do but also to decide which thoughts and words he will think and speak and which he will refrain from. Yet the Jewish person has the potential for even more. This is because the Jewish soul receives a direct inflow of the primal divine light, or spiritual energy, emanating from God's being. The energy of divine will that thus enters the Jewish person empowers him to exercise the same willpower as God, its source: a causative and active will rising from the depths of himself. The rest of Creation, though, receives divine energy only as *reflected off* the Jewish soul—its source of energy is thus not primary and causative but *reactive*. So all other beings and phenomena are not the ultimate authors of their actions but are bound in some way to *reactive* behavior because the essence of their willpower is reactive.

APPENDIX C

ACTUALIZING HUMAN FREE WILL

 od called out to Adam, "Where are you?" (Genesis 3:9).

A radical change had just taken place in human nature, an awesome spiritual fall from *Gan Eden* into the depths of Hell—a subordination of human nature to baser drives. Man's noble nature—his soul, the very essence of his being—was now so lost and hidden that God Himself had to call out to him, "Where are you?"

The average human being, when confronted with a distressing situation, will be troubled and find it difficult to keep his cheer. When in a joyous situation he will celebrate and not easily become distressed. This being so, a human being has become nothing more than a clearinghouse for all the passing thoughts that reflect what's happening in his world—he himself, though, the soul of his being, is not there.

Keep track for a day of the thoughts that pass through your mind and see if they are not just thoughts of external, frequently current events. As those events change, so too will those thoughts. Presently, most thoughts are worrisome, but with God's help, when the world situation improves, more cheerful thoughts will come to mind.

But neither the previous worrisome thoughts nor the future cheerful ones are the essence of the human being—they are just migrant squatters passing through. The previous ones were like irksome aliens and the later ones will be a boon. There is a constant turnover depending on the day and what's going on in the person's world. But "Where are you?"—where is your *real* self? Because when a person is fully present and at home at his deepest being, then neither will joy intoxicate his consciousness nor will distress disturb his calm.

Now to create this inner sanctum and make it the control center of one's inner world, not to be a victim to external circumstances that trigger thoughts through the mind's open door, one must become infused by and inspired with a divine source of spiritual energy. The source of this energy, though, is not something that can be grasped intellectually—it must be experienced by oneself. Nevertheless, lest you ask how can God demand of you something that He is not revealing to you and you yourself have no clue what it is, let me try to explain it with a metaphor. When there is a fire, God forbid, a person gets a sudden surge of superhuman energy. At other times, try as he may, he cannot accomplish the heroic feats he did during the fire. Where did all this energy come from?

Let us proceed. This physical world is nothing but a material manifestation of higher spiritual worlds—it has no inherent essence of its own. As above, so below—our world is only a map. Now God, the One, created one amorphous cosmic matter—not many pre-patterned ones. But God made many conceptual forms (spiritual in nature) to give a diversity of design to this uniform mass and to fashion it with features we will be able to grasp. Nevertheless, it is only like filtering the sun's light so that we are able to look straight at it—it is still the primal essence of the sun and its rays that we are seeing. This is what our world is like: there is one cosmic substance and many forms and qualities that it can take. A form is anything that can be seen or felt by any of the senses of sight, sound, or touch.

Now every form has the power to draw all its needs from the concentrated energy stored in the stuff of creation in order to sustain itself. A seed contains no germinal tree or leaves, yet all this grows from it. Why will the seed not grow to a tree if it is not planted in the ground and if it does not receive all the air and water it needs? Because the seed is only a form with the potential to draw out hidden energies contained in the singular ground of existence and to manifest them in its particular form. Similarly, a human being: if a newborn baby does not receive the life energy it needs from the world in the physical form of food, drink, and air, it will not be able to grow.

In summation, everything that we see in this world is not unique primal matter but only one manifest form of the common stuff of creation, and this form has the power to draw energy from that common ground of existence and express it in its unique form.

Now, since one of the characteristics of the human form is unlimited free choice, human energy must then also be limitless. In other words, if someone decides that suddenly he needs more energy, his form will draw that extra energy from the endless amount stored in cosmic matter, as in our previous example of the fire. No human being can foretell his potential states of consciousness and physical energy because they are limitless, just as his consciousness itself is only bound by his free will. This is not to say that anyone can become a Samson—we are mainly talking about human consciousness and will-power as opposed to one's physical self. This is because free choice takes place in consciousness and will, so into them one can draw added energy. One can even become more intelligent than the quota allotted him at conception (*Niddah* 16b)—we see that dull people who sincerely devote their efforts can attain higher levels of wisdom and sophistication. The driving force behind this is the burning sense of need that he feels to attain the wisdom that is as strong as the pain of need one feels to save one's house from burning. This is the meaning of "He who increases wisdom increases pain" (Ecclesiastes 1:18). There can be no increase in consciousness, in wisdom, without a preceding increase in the pain caused by experiencing its lack.

This all applies to consciousness and will, which are the seat of one's free choice. Physical levels of energy, though, are much more difficult to raise. Only someone whose consciousness and will are in full control of his body can draw more energy into his system. Because his consciousness and willpower are unlimited, having actualized this charactistic of the human form, he is able to perform this feat. During a fire, the average person can do this because his urgent will then takes control of his body, which is then energized to the heroic feat.

This explains why we see physically weak saintly

people who are able to accomplish great spiritual acts that require such levels of energy even a Samson could not match. And in general, even the average Jewish person cannot foretell his potential energy for spiritual feats—the simplest of people would never be able to accomplish any other time during the year what he does in preparation for Pesach. He neither has the energy nor can he find enough time. This is because the necessity and desire to perform this service now fill his consciousness and willpower and take control of his body. The latter, with their free will, then channel into his physical system a greater amount of energy.

The same principle applies for all spiritual feats. If a person's consciousness and willpower become so single-minded in reaching this goal, so much so that he has almost lost his free choice—he *must* do this, and this drive overruns his whole self—then he will find whatever strength and time it takes. But someone who is stuck at the fork in the road of life, who is always in a state of indecision—shall he pursue spiritual goals or not? He has never made up his mind—such a person will never find the time or strength in his life for these things because willpower comes only with decision. Even when he "wants" to pursue these goals, his body lacks the energy and will not listen.

This gives us a new insight into the two questions posed to a person after his lifetime: "Have you set aside time for Torah study? Have you been fruitful?" (*Shabbat* 31a). As explained in other sources (*Likkutey Moharan* I:284), the question is to a busy person, and with our introduction perhaps the two questions are one: "Have you 'stolen' time from your *busy*ness and made that time 'fruitful'—that is, have you created more time and strength than you thought you had?"

Let us now return to the first point: this world that

we see as separate entities has no real existence of its own—it is only the manifestation of the great one cosmic matter in all different shapes and forms. Now the Jewish person whose human form is endowed with absolute free will should be able to draw infinite amounts of energy at his will. Let, then, the Jewish person meditate deeply on this:

> Somewhere there is the Infinite Source . . . the root of all that is holy and pure . . . greater than Creation, a light of absolute truth . . . the Source of true life beyond limitation. . . . Why am I so distant from this Source? . . . Why am I so empty, so lowly and dry? . . . Why am I so unholy and unpure?

A passion for the holy will be aroused at the core of your being, a passion that will energize your entire body. And because the human form can draw to itself unlimited power with its will, it can draw from this Infinite Source—not only from the spiritual energy that is contained in Creation but also from that which hovers around it.

When such intense spiritual energy enters the human system, the body becomes shaken and numb—the ego shell is shattered and the person is transformed into someone else. He experiences things that he could not before and yearns for things he did not until then. He may even then attain divine inspiration.

It is not inevitable, though, that he be moved to unusual bodily movements. True, sometimes when very aroused one may be unable to restrain himself from spontaneous surging of vocal or bodily expression, but this is not the acid test for arousal. The main manifestation of all this spiritual energy is in the depths of the person's heart. The person has "exploded" from this intense energy level that has burst into the core of his soul.

This gives us a bit of understanding into the dynamics of spiritual energies in terms we can relate to.

And this is the difference between one who draws to himself extra energy with his free will and someone who is sufficed with his standard quota—the latter has virtually lost his human form. Animals and plants also derive their needs from existing matter, and the human ability for thought and worldly aspiration does not make him any different. The quintessence of the human form, that which defines him as different from all other creatures, is his ability to draw energy at will. As long as one has not actualized his form, he cannot really be called a human being—he has yet to enter his inner sanctum and take control of his inner world.

But as we have said before, in order to arouse a burning drive, you must first be aware of what you lack. Now compared to the infinite that surrounds us, we are only infinitely empty. So when God called out to Adam, "Where are you?—you are so empty," Adam confessed his mistake: "I heard Your voice . . . and I was awed— lo, I am naked so I hid." Adam was saying, "I thought I was wise and had the prerequisite to wisdom—awe of God. But since I thought that I lack nothing but am wise when I am really 'naked,' so I 'hid'—I hid from myself, from my awesome power of free will, and lo, I remained spiritually naked. Rather than drawing spiritual energy to myself to strengthen my control of my life, I have remained a doormat to the outside world and have remained hidden from myself."

Drawing this spiritual energy is difficult because it hovers around Creation from above and beyond it. But once one person has brought it into the world, it will be easier for someone else to obtain it—the energy is already in "circulation." This is the work of a Master for his students.

APPENDIX D

TOPICAL TABLE OF CONTENTS

Topics are listed by entry number.

Spiritual guidance 1–48

Insights into human nature
4, 6, 7, 9, 10, 14, 16, 23, 25, 33, 41, 44, 45,
Appendix A, B, C

Prayer
4, 18, 19, 30, 31, 35

Meditations and visualizations
xxix, 2, 4, 13, 18, 22, 24, 26, 27, 28, 29, 30, 34, 37,
40, 43, 46, 47, 48, Appendix C

EDITOR'S NOTES

p. xv	line 9	As reprinted in the *Sefer Zikaron le'Rebbe mi'Paesetzna* (Jerusalem, 1993), p. 88.
p. xviii	line 30	Entry 7. See also entry 10.
p. xviii	line 34	Ibid.
p. xxi	line 15	This was Rabbi Chaim Kreizworth, now chief rabbi of Antwerp, then a staff lecturer in Rebbe Kalonymus' *yeshivah*.
p xxi	line 19	Rebbe Kalonymus explained that just as on Yom Kippur one must fast no matter how difficult, so too on Purim one must rejoice no matter how difficult.

p. xxi	line 31	See entry 1.
p. xxii	line 20	*Ya'arot Dvash* II:11, p. 183, in the Jerusalem, 1983, edition.
p. xxii	line 26	See Appendix C.
p. xxvi	line 3	The journal manuscript found in this container was only up to entry 35—the remaining entries, 36 to 48, are from a different journal. But since the Rebbe's heirs printed them together in this format, I have also done so.
p. xxix	line 12	Translated from *Derekh HaMelekh* (Rabbi Kalonymus' *Shabbat* discourses) (Jerusalem, 5751), pp. 406–407.
p. xxix	line 31	See journal entry 45.
p. xxx	line 21	See journal entry 33.
p. xxxv	line 4	*Hakhsharat HaAvrekhim.*
p. xxxv	line 5	*M'vo HaShearim*, part of *Chovat HaAvrekhim.*
p. xxxv	line 6	*Tzav V'Ziruz.*
p. 2	line 11	See also entry 12.
p. 11	line 34	See also entries 15, 38.
p. 14	line 23	See also entry 20.
p. 17	line 14	See *Shevet Musar* chap. 25 from *Nedarim.*
p. 23	line 9	Even in this, though, one must be careful that the emotional sensation not become the goal and prayer and Torah learning only a means to it. Here is what Rebbe Kalonymus once said to a group of students who came to

him before Yom Kippur for spiritual stimulation:

> Human nature is to be drawn to hear sensational stories and to be driven to listen to dramatic news. This is because these things tickle a person's very being, nearly making the heart jump from its place. For the very same reason people are driven to drink liquor: they enjoy the tingling sensation that it gives them deep inside. And this is also why people may love to listen to inspirational talks. So because you want the stimulation of alcoholic beverage, is it then my task to serve as your drinks?

And the students were indeed more shaken than they would have been by any other talk.

Rebbe Kalonymus' teaching here also explains the mindless human craving to read thrilling novels.

p. 23   line 13   See also entry 11.
p. 27   line 13   Rebbe Kalonymus is stating here quite clearly that free choice is not an inherent given of the human condition—it is a spiritual level to strive for. This idea is borne out by Rabbi Yonah of

Gerondi in *Shaarei Teshuvah* III:17, where he states that the loftiest spiritual levels have been transmitted to us in the medium of positive commandments. Even before listing the commandments of studying God's ways; trusting in Him; contemplating His greatness and loving - kindness; purity; awe and love of God and holding His everpresence in consciousness, Rabbi Yonah mentions free choice. As Rebbe Kalonymus says here, it is indeed the prerequisite to everything. For more of Rebbe Kalonymus on free choice, see his essays in Appendixes B and C.

p. 29	line 12	See also entry 9.
p. 31	line 11	See also entry 1.
p. 38	line 6	See also Appendix A.
p. 39	line 10	See also entry 41.
p. 48	line 7	See entry 4.
p. 66	line 24	To add another dimension to Rebbe Kalonymus' inner dialogue, here is what Rabbi Yisrael Hopstein o.b.m., the saintly Maggid Koznitz, says in his commentary on *Avot* 1:6:

> Sometimes a person gets a spontaneous thought to serve God in a certain way—this thought actually comes from God and is His

will for that person at that time. But sometimes the person will evade the call and try to ignore the thought. This is what the *Mishnah* is telling us, "Make for yourself a master": realize that these thoughts are sent by God to guide you—follow them rather than evade them. Make God for your Master, as we find that He is called a Master. We see this from the blessing "He Who teaches Torah to His People, Israel." How true this is. God is always teaching us His Torah and the way He desires us to serve Him. We could not have any thought if it did not come from Him. Once in history, this phenomenon was very evident—when He gave us the Torah on Mount Sinai. Nevertheless, also ever since, a certain ray of illumination enters our minds to guide us. Therefore, whatever thought of divine service comes to mind—this is how God wants you now to serve Him.

p. 99   line 7   Rabbi Kalonymus elucidates on this concept in Appendix B.

p. 100   line 29   Rabbi Kalonymus elucidates on this concept in Appendix B.

p. 103   line 9   Rebbe Kalonymus wrote "we" rather than "they" for the doctors because, as we mentioned in the introduction, with his knowledge of medicine and surgery, he was probably very involved in the decision to operate.

p. 112   line 11   *Shalosh Seudos* was a time of profound spiritual experience for Rebbe Kalonymus (see 26 and 47) and to have had the vision of this happening at *Shalosh Seudos* must indeed have been deeply moving. We may even conjecture that it was the feelings of faith and encouragement associated with *Shalosh Seudos* that sparked this vision for the Rebbe.

p. 118   line 10   Here ends the text of Rebbe Kalonymus' journal manuscript found buried beneath the Warsaw Ghetto. From here to the end is the text of another journal kept by the Rebbe. See the introduction.

p. 124   line 15   See also Appendix A.

p. 149   line 2   Appendix A was translated from *M'vo HaShearim,* chap. 10, pp. 57b–59a.

p. 150   line 15   The soul fills the body, and God fills the world. Both see and are not seen, sustain that which they fill, are pure, and can be found only in the innermost worlds of deep experience *(Berakhot* 10a). See also *Leviticus Rabbah* 4:8.

p. 155   line 3   Appendix B was translated from *M'Vo HaShearim,* chap. 3, pp. 20b–21a.

p. 156   line 34   In other words, the Jewish soul alone is that which is in God's "innermost room" and absorbs and reflects the primal divine light. All other things receive only a reflection of the Jewish soul. If God is denoted by the sun and the Jewish soul by the moon, then the night side of the planet Earth is the rest of Creation.

p. 157   line 32   The relevant application of all this is that though, practically speaking, most people *are* severely limited in their free will due to the powerful force of habit, learned reactions, and early-life programming, nevertheless, there *is* the potential to transcend it all by tapping into deep inner resources of will. This is done, as we can gather from Rebbe Kalonymus, by completely opening up to and surrendering to God's will.

p. 159   line 2   Appendix C was translated from *Derekh HaMelekh* (Rebbe Kalonymus' *Shabbat* discourses) (Jerusalem, 5751), pp. 421–423.

p. 164   line 25   *Ruach HaKodesh* in the original.

INDEX OF PASSAGES

GENERAL INDEX

Roman numerals refer to front matter. Arabic numbers refer to entry and page span in which index entries can be found.

spiritual progress
requires, 38:123–124
Inner silence, achievement
of, xxix-xxxii
Inner voices
answering of negative,
27:65–68, 30:73–78
irrational, 33:91–93
Intentions, pure and
ulterior, 44:135–137
Irrational thoughts, human
nature, 33:91–93

Jew
becoming a simple,
19:45–46
motions of, in divine
service, 31:79–87
simple holy acts of,
27:65–68
Jewish People
collective soul of,
30:73–78
coronation of God,
34:95–102
God's secret palace,
34:95–102
God's throne of glory,
34:95–102
rejoicing of, 30:73–78
souls of, reflected in
heavenly bodies,
34:95–102
tears and suffering of,
34:95–102
Jewish survival, xxi. *See
also* Estranged Jews

Journal keeping, as way to
gain posterity, 1:1–2

Kol Nidre, 26:61–63

Levites, music played by, in
Temple, 35:103–118
Life
celebration of, 34:95–102
efficient and productive,
42:131
entire, passes through
memory before
death, 40:127–128
inner, taking possession
of, 20:47–49
simple and primal drive
for, 44:135–137
transitions in, 19:45–46
vows and, 42:131
Light
bodies of, reflect Jewish
souls, 34:95–102
waves dance for joy,
34:95–102
Love of God, meditation
and, xxxi

Medicine, Kalonymus
Kalman and, xiv-xvi
Meditation
act of, xxx-xxxi
clearing the mind of
distraction, 22:53
inner silence,
introduction
levels of experience,
28:69–70

Remorse
  evoking of deep,
    40:127–128
  over past life before
    death, 40:127–128
  productive and
    nonproductive, 6:17
Resolution, self-wishing
  versus, in spiritual
  progress, 14:35–36
Rich man story, 39:125–126

Sadness, over unfulfilled
  wish, 3:5–6
Sages of Great Assembly,
  31:79–87 *note*
Seclusion, for meditative
  prayer, 4:7–14,
  18:43–44
Sefer HaIkkarim,
  45:139–141
Sefer Torah, dedication
  ceremony of, 27:65–68
Self
  development of unique
  free choice and,
    10:25–27
  spiritual progress and,
    38:123–124
  sense of, separates us
    from God,
    45:139–141
  self-awareness, of
    thoughts, 33:91–93
  self-control, versus
    healing the soul,
    4:7–14

self-deception, 1:1–2,
  3:5–6, 4:7–14,
  34:95–102,
  40:127–128
self-esteem, low,
  25:59–60
self-fulfillment, all
  thoughts revolve
  around,
  44:135–137
self-talk
  irrational, 33:91–93
  of the soul,
    34:95–102
  spotting and
    changing,
    33:91–93
Shalosh Seudos
  fear of facing God after
    death during,
    17:41–42
  inspiration at
  like at *Kol Nidre,*
    26:61–63
  like on Yom Kippur,
    47:145–146
  vision of, 35:103–118
Shapira, Kalonymus Kalman
  aspires to write many
    books, 42:131
  birth of, xii
  childhood of, xii-xiii,
    35:103–118
  chosen rebbe, xvi
  death of, xxi
  death of family members,
    xx

ABOUT THE EDITOR

After many years of talmudic study, Yehoshua Starrett's spiritual searching brought him into the deeper dimensions of chasidic teachings. In his previous books, *The Breslov Haggadah* and *Esther: A Breslov Commentary on the Megillah,* he weaves together chasidic thought and psychological insight. Starrett lives with his wife and children in Jerusalem, where he continues to learn, teach, and write.